NEWMAN'S
BIRDS
BY COLOUR

This book is dedicated to all fledgling birders.

NEWMAN'S
BIRDS
BY COLOUR

KENNETH NEWMAN

in association with

Irene Bredenkamp and Phoebus Perdikis

Struik Publishers
(a division of New Holland Publishing (South Africa) (Pty) Ltd)
Cornelis Struik House, 80 McKenzie Street, Cape Town, 8001

New Holland Publishing is a member of Johnnic Communications Ltd.
Visit us at **www.struik.co.za**

www.imagesofafrica.co.za

IMAGES OF AFRICA
P H O T O   L I B R A R Y

First published 2000

5 7 9 10 8 6 4

Project Co-ordinator: Reneé Ferreira
Editor: Pearson Editorial
Designer: Lyndall du Toit
Cover Design: Janice Evans
Proofreader and Indexer: Hilda van Ryswyk

Concept: Irene Bredenkamp and Phoebus Perdikis
Reproduction by Hirt & Carter Cape (Pty) Ltd, Cape Town
Printed and bound by Kyodo Printing Co (Singapore) Pte Ltd

ISBN 1 86872 448 4

Also available in Afrikaans as
VOËLS VOLGENS KLEUR

Contents

KEY TO IDENTIFICATION

WHAT'S ALL THIS ABOUT?

This book has been designed primarily as a guide for beginner birdwatchers and all those, a little higher up the birding ladder, who continue to struggle with getting to know some common birds. Time and again I am told, 'It flew away before I could get a better look at it, but it was *red*' (or blue, or green or yellow). Invariably others who saw the bird will argue about its colour or exactly where on the bird the colour was. Much time will be spent paging through the field guide, from albatrosses to canaries, but to no avail. Rather than accepting the motto 'A bird flown is seldom known', the disgruntled birder will suffer a restless night. What can be done?

There is little doubt that the features memorised by most novice birders in the above circumstances are the bird's approximate size and its colour, or the colour that made an impression. There is no doubt whatsoever that colour, no matter how briefly glimpsed, remains in the memory. If one is to assume that the bird seen was indeed red, then the list of possible species will be very short indeed. However, when one delves a little deeper into the problem, it usually transpires that, on second thoughts, it was only its beak, head or tail that was red (or was it green?). In retrospect the observer is never quite certain. At this point the 'expert' is expected to produce the correct answer and put everyone out of their misery.

My co-authors experienced these identification problems on many occasions and so the germ of an idea was born. After many months and much homework, Irene had cut to pieces numerous copies of *Newman's Birds of Southern Africa* to assemble a weighty paste-up collection of birds by colour. This eventually arrived on my publisher's desk. And so the idea began to take shape.

Birds by Colour focuses on birds that have a dominant colour in their plumage, beaks or legs. It is not a field guide and was never intended to be, but should be regarded as a companion to my field guide *Newman's Birds of Southern Africa*.

Kenneth Newman

A flash of crimson disappeared into a thorn tree.

HOW TO USE THIS BOOK

This book has been planned with a dual purpose. The first section gives aspirant birders a broad overview of what makes a bird a 'bird' as opposed to other animals, and a glimpse of the way birds live. The section touches on flight, migration, feeding, display, nests and bird habitats. It is written without scientific jargon, to introduce the novice to birds as fascinating living beings. This is followed by notes on identifying birds; how to start; what you need, and where to look for them.

The second section is designed to help the beginner identify 'the one that got away'; a briefly seen, tantalizing feathered creature that flew before you could focus but left a lasting colour impression. Let's say you've seen an unidentified bird and retained an impression of its predominant colour, say red. You can now page to the section dealing with red birds and see if you can find the bird there. Once the bird has been 'found' in this book by its colour, refer to *Newman's Birds of Southern Africa* to confirm your identification. Once you have located the bird in the index of Newman's field guide, ascertain from the distribution map on the relevant page that the bird you think you saw occurs in the region and that it is present at the appropriate time of the year, plus all the other information about the species that will help confirm the accuracy of your identification.

Common English name.

Colour tab works with the colour bar to identify the colour section you are in.

Colour bar works in conjunction with side colour tabs to identify the colour section.

Text isolates first the typical habitat in which the bird occurs, then the dominant identification features of the bird.

Afrikaans name.

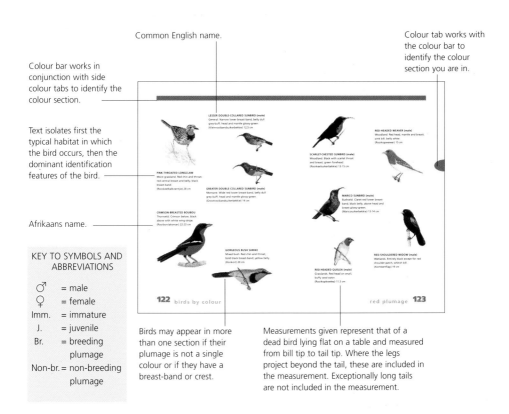

KEY TO SYMBOLS AND ABBREVIATIONS

♂ = male
♀ = female
Imm. = immature
J. = juvenile
Br. = breeding plumage
Non-br. = non-breeding plumage

Birds may appear in more than one section if their plumage is not a single colour or if they have a breast-band or crest.

Measurements given represent that of a dead bird lying flat on a table and measured from bill tip to tail tip. Where the legs project beyond the tail, these are included in the measurement. Exceptionally long tails are not included in the measurement.

WHAT IS A BIRD?

It is not enough simply to say a bird is a creature that flies. In fact not all birds can fly, whereas some reptiles, fish and even mammals do fly. Certain lizards have thin membranes stretched between their legs which act as simple wings, while some frogs have enlarged feet with webs between their toes. These simple 'air foils' merely enable the creatures to descend through the air slowly. In other words they are gliders; they cannot flap their 'air foils' to fly higher. We all know about flying fish with their significantly enlarged fins that resemble wings, but once the fish has jumped out of the water its flight is merely a delayed descent back again. An important exception to these delayed descents is one group of mammals: the bats. Like birds, bats are able to fly and manoeuvre at great speed, the membranes between their front and rear legs being well developed and stiffened by bones. This modification enables these membranes to be flapped like wings to propel the bat over long distances.

The one important structural difference that characterises a bird is its unique covering of feathers. The first bird discovered in fossilised form, known as Archaeopterix, was a creature somewhere between a reptile and a bird as we know it. Archaeopterix had teeth in its beak and a long reptilian tail, but it was entirely covered in feathers and could fly. Feathers are believed to be a modification of reptilian scales. They take various forms, from contour feathers to the very important flight feathers. Read about them in the section entitled 'feather structure'.

Archaeopterix, the first true bird,
lived about 140 million years ago.

THE CLASSIFICATION OF BIRDS

Although we do not use scientific names for birds in this book, every bird (and other known creatures and plants) has a scientific name in addition to the common names that we use in the various languages. When common names are used internationally they often cause confusion, since names used elsewhere can be quite different from those we use among ourselves in southern Africa. For example, we are familiar with birds such as louries, mousebirds and dikkops, but in much of Africa and even in the rest of the world these birds are known as turacos, colies and thick-knees! The same sort of local naming takes place in other countries too, and there are no rules to prevent it. It is therefore important to have a standardised set of names for all living things to prevent any possibility of confusion. The international system for scientific names is used by all countries whatever their home language. Under this system all living things are given two-part names using a neutral language: Latin or Ancient Greek. No two birds can have the same scientific name and once the name has been allocated it cannot easily be changed.

Birds are grouped into families, and within the families are one or more genera (genus in the singular). Each genus has within it one or more species. A species can be further divided into subspecies. For example, the common House Sparrow belongs to the family Ploceidae. Within that family one finds the genus *Passer*, and within that genus the House Sparrow has been given the specific name *domesticus*. The House Sparrow's official name is *Passer domesticus* throughout the world and it is always written in italic type. This particular sparrow originated in Europe but, over the years, its range spread into Asia, Africa and even farther afield. Some of these far-flung populations of the House Sparrow developed changes in size and plumage details. Ultimately they came to be regarded as subspecies of the original or nominate European race and were given an additional subspecific name. As a result, the Indian race of the House Sparrow is known as *Passer domesticus indicus* and it is this subspecies that was introduced, and eventually became dominant, in South Africa. There are three other sparrows in South Africa, all belonging to the genus *Passer*. They are the Cape Sparrow *P. melanurus,* the Great Sparrow *P. motitensis* and the Southern Grey-headed Sparrow *P. diffusus.* While all scientific bird names are written in italic type, only the first or generic name is given a capital initial.

What is a species?

A species is best defined as a type of bird that can only reproduce with other members of its kind. For example, we have discussed four species of sparrow that live in southern Africa. Although all four belong to the genus *Passer,* under normal circumstances the four species will not interbreed.

During courtship, species are prevented from interbreeding in various natural ways. Voice certainly plays an important role. Although we may not detect any great difference between the voice of, say, the Cape Sparrow and the Great Sparrow, there are in fact many subtle differences in structure and pitch that are quite clear to the birds themselves. Another important factor is plumage colour. The marks and colours seen in birds play an important role in courtship and territorial defence. For example, the black markings on the heads and breasts of both the male Cape and Great Sparrows each have a different pattern and these are important recognition features for the female, as is the distribution of the chestnut plumage colouring in the males. Voice, plumage and the male's unique courtship behaviour all combine to ensure specific isolation.

THE ANATOMY OF A BIRD

Getting to know the names of the various parts of a bird is necessary if you are to understand the terminology used in discussing birds in your fieldguide. You may wonder, for instance, why the White-fronted Bee-eater is so called when it obviously doesn't have a white breast, but if you check the anatomy diagram you will see that the 'front' of a bird is not its chest but its forehead. Likewise, terms such as secondaries, primaries, coverts, tarsus and orbital ring need to be understood. I recommend that you give yourself 15 minutes to study the external 'Anatomy of a Bird' chart below and thereafter refer to it from time to time just to refresh your memory.

ANATOMY OF A BIRD

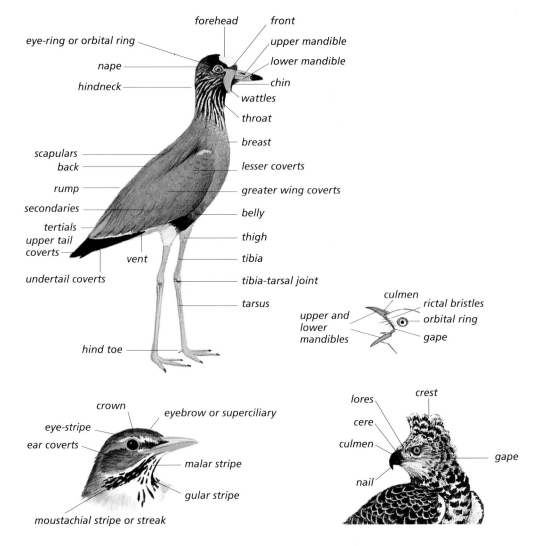

WHAT IS A PASSERINE?

Passerines, also known as songbirds or perching birds, consist of about 5 200 species and make up more than 50% of the roughly 9 000 bird species found in the world. Passerines are land birds and typical members of this group are the robins, thrushes, white-eyes and wagtails that frequent our gardens. They are all small- to medium-sized birds, the largest passerines being the crow family. The most important external feature of a passerine bird is its four toes, all set at the same level: three toes facing forward and one toe directed backward, all unwebbed. This standard foot arrangement of passerines is crucial to their perching ability. Have you ever wondered why these little birds don't get blown off their perches while roosting on a windy night? It's because their feet actually lock onto the perch while the bird is crouched sleeping, and only relax and unlock when the bird flexes its legs by standing (see the diagram below).

The typical passerine foot has all four toes joined at the same level, three facing forward and one at the back.

A SIMPLIFIED DIAGRAM OF A PERCHING FOOT

To settle securely on a small branch or slender wire, the bird's flexion leg-tendons are automatically tightened as the leg is folded.

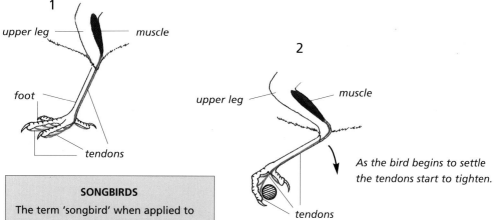

1
upper leg — muscle
foot
tendons

2
upper leg — muscle

As the bird begins to settle the tendons start to tighten.

tendons

3

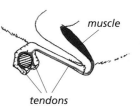

muscle

When the leg is fully folded the toes are locked onto the perch and can only be unlocked when the bird stands.

tendons

SONGBIRDS

The term 'songbird' when applied to passerines is not entirely accurate. Although most of the world's finest songsters are passerines, there are also some very pleasant sounds uttered by non-passerines, such as the pleasant duet of Black-collared Barbets or the soft cooing of a Laughing Dove.

Non-passerines

The remaining feathered creatures are ocean birds, inland waterbirds, bustards, francolins, raptors, sandgrouse, doves and pigeons, cuckoos, coucals, parrots, nightjars, swifts, bee-eaters, kingfishers, barbets, honeyguides, woodpeckers, rollers, hoopoes and hornbills. These birds do not have locking feet like passerines, but you will notice that some have long legs (inland waterbirds and grassland birds) while others have very short legs (terns, swifts, nightjars, wood hoopoes). A closer look will reveal the great variety of leg lengths and foot shapes shared by this group. Some plovers, dikkops, coursers, oystercatchers and bustards have no hind toe. In those that do, the hind toe is often small and may be placed higher up the leg than the front toes. Another variable feature of non-passerines is the great variety of beak shapes and lengths seen in this group, from the very long beaks of some waterbirds to the heavy appearance of those carried by hornbills.

BIRDS' LEGS AND FEET

We see very little of the true leg in most birds because the upper sections, the bird's 'knee' and tibia, are covered by feathers. What we see as the backward-bending 'knee' is equivalent to our ankle joint, while the lower 'leg' is actually the ankle. Technically then, a bird's foot extends from what we see as the 'knee' (the tibio-tarsal joint) down to the toes.

In some long-legged non-passerine birds, for example storks and flamingoes, quite a lot of the 'upper leg' or tibia is exposed, but in the majority of passerines it is either fully or partially covered by feathers. Again the total leg length of a bird varies enormously in relation to its body size, from the very long legs of the Secretarybird to the extremely short legs of a swift or a nightjar. Birds that need to run at speed, such as the Ostrich and other terrestrial species, need long legs, whereas aerial feeders, which have little need to walk, have the shortest legs.

In birds' feet we again see great variation. Birds of prey have very powerful feet, especially the inner and rear toes, which are used for grasping and holding. Their talons are also large, well curved and very sharp. A similar foot with short toes and sharp claws is found in parrots, but in their case the foot is used for clinging and scrambling along branches, often in strange attitudes, to reach fruit. The foot is then used as a hand for feeding.

Certain waterbirds that need to walk on floating vegetation have long toes to enable them to do so by spreading their weight over a greater area. The African Jacana has the longest

> **PADDLE-FEET**
> Ducks have webbed, paddle-like feet as an aid to swimming, but cormorants and many other waterbirds also have webbed feet. The Dabchick, Red-knobbed Coot and African Finfoot have semi-webbed or lobed feet that serve a similar purpose. Some webbed or semi-webbed feet, as found in flamingoes, storks and avocets, serve a dual purpose, allowing the bird to walk on soft mud and to swim.

An African Jacana showing a long-toed foot as it approaches its nest with eggs.

W. Tarboton

toes of all, plus greatly elongated claws. In contrast, swifts have very small feet with all four toes facing forward – an arrangement that, coupled with their sharp needle-like claws, enables them to cling to the rough surfaces of rocky cliffs (or buildings) where they roost and nest. Swifts cannot perch on trees or telephone wires like swallows.

A highly specialised foot is that of the flightless Ostrich, with only two toes, one large and the other small, designed for fast running. Perhaps the strangest foot of all also has the strangest name: the zygodactyl or yoke-toed foot found in woodpeckers, barbets, cuckoos, parrots and others. In this foot the toes are permanently paired, two in front and two behind, the first and fourth toes pointing backward to ensure a very firm grip. Adaptations of the zygodactyl foot are found in kingfishers, hornbills and rollers, where the third and fourth toes are joined: the syndactyl foot.

THE LEGS OF A SWIFT
The legs of swifts are so short that they can barely walk on a flat surface. If they were to settle on the ground by accident they could only shuffle and, with their combination of short legs and enormously long wings, would be unable to flap sufficiently to fly away unless a strong wind was blowing. Because of this, swifts spend their lives flying, unless they are roosting or nesting. They cannot perch.

An Alpine Swift

introduction **13**

EXAMPLES OF SPECIALISED FEET

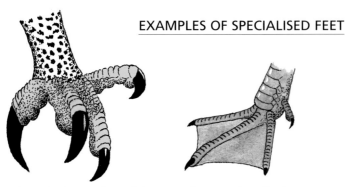

The Ostrich has only two toes; an adaption for fast running.

The typical raptor foot of the Crowned Eagle. The powerful talons are adapted for gripping.

The Cape Shoveller, in common with most ducks, has the front three toes joined by webs.

The Red-knobbed Coot has a lobed foot in contrast with the webbed feet of ducks.

The African Jacana has greatly elongated toes and claws which distribute its weight while walking on floating vegetation.

Woodpeckers have two toes' facing backwards; a good arrangement for climbing on trees.

Swifts have all four toes facing forward for clinging to rough surfaces. They cannot perch.

BEAKS AND BILLS

BEAK OR BILL?
The words 'beak' and 'bill' are synonymous. This author uses both as a personal choice: beak for the smaller ones and bill for the larger. In fact, there are no rules unless one wishes to get technical, in which case we refer to the bird's 'rostrum'.

In general usage we refer to a bird's bill (or beak) as being two separate extensions of its jaw: the upper and lower 'mandibles' (see 'Anatomy of a Bird' on page 10). The upper ridge of the upper mandible, extending from the tip to the bird's forehead, is called the 'culmen'. The region where the two mandibles join (the corner of the mouth) is known as the 'gape'. The young of many small birds that are still dependent on their parents for food have the soft gape coloured creamy, yellow or orange.

In birds of prey, parrots and pigeons the base of the upper mandible, surrounding the nostrils, is soft and thickened, forming a 'cere'. In birds of prey the cere is often yellow in colour, while in parrots and pigeons it is usually grey. Many

Swifts are by far the most aerial of birds; so much so that at least one species remains airborne for a year or more. This is the European or Northern Swift *Apus apus*, which visits southern Africa during the northern winter, when the birds are not breeding.

When at home in their northern breeding grounds these swifts tend to breed in church towers, houses and other buildings where they are able to fly directly into the nest site. At worst they will alight on the wall or parapet, where they cling briefly before shuffling to the nest on their minute legs. Their nesting period, egg-laying, incubation and young-rearing lasts approximately seven weeks after which the parents take to the air again where they probably remain until the following breeding period some 10 months later. Once the young bird has left its nest it does not return to it but joins its parents' flock. If by the following breeding season the young bird is not ready to breed it will probably remain airborne for another year. It seems that at night these swifts rise to a great height and are able to sleep, or 'cat-nap', on the wing.

In parrots and some raptors the cere is grey, but in the Feral Pigeon (left) it is whitish and swollen in appearance. On the right is a Wahlberg's Eagle, showing its yellow cere.

THE FEEDING ACTION OF THE GREATER FLAMINGO

Flamingoes are filter-feeders on microscopic blue algae found in soda lakes and salt lagoons. The brilliant pink plumage of flamingoes is derived from this diet. To feed, the peculiar bill with its very small, lid-like upper mandible is held inverted beneath the surface.

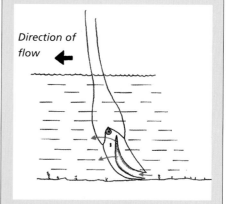

Direction of flow

Fine, brush-like projections called 'lamellae' fringe the inside of the of the flamingo's upper and lower mandibles, and act as sieves to catch the microscopic algae on which the bird feeds. Water is taken into the bill by a pumping action of the tongue and sieved through the lamellae to retain the algae before being expelled.

seabirds have long, tubular nostrils, either paired or singular, that extend along the culmen. These extended nostrils, or 'nares', serve to conduct the excretion of surplus salt and seawater, ingested with their food, from the seabird's system.

Soft swellings or knobs are seen on the upper mandible of the male Knob-billed Duck and, to a lesser extent, on the bill of the male Spur-winged Goose. The function of these knobs is not known. Others have functional additions to their culmens, such

as the horny casques carried by many hornbills and well demonstrated in the bill of the Trumpeter Hornbill. These lightweight casques are hollow and probably act as 'resonance' boxes to increase the volume and carrying power of the bird's voice. They are usually largest in the male bird.

Whether a bird has a small beak or a large bill, the reason for its size and shape will be found in the bird's food and feeding habits. Knowing this is a sure guide to the type of bird it is.

There are many birds that feed only while flying; these are the swifts, swallows, nightjars and bee-eaters. Swifts are powerful flyers and are able to cover great distances on their long, scimitar-shaped wings to avoid bad weather. They feed on airborne insects and spiders, often called 'aerial plankton', which they catch in their wide mouths while flying. Swallows feed in much the same way as swifts, but they are entirely unrelated: swallows are passerines while swifts are non-passerines. Swallows' legs, though fairly short, enable them to walk when necessary, as they must do when collecting mud for nest-building. Swallows, and their close relatives the martins, are not as rapid on the wing as swifts, their flight action being more leisurely. Nightjars are strictly nocturnal aerial feeders, lying up by day among leaves on the ground, or on a branch or rock according to their specific behaviour. Nightjars also have very wide gapes, but have, in addition, stiff 'rictal' bristles surrounding them, which serve as a sort of catching net for moths and other night flying insects that make up their diet.

This close up of a nightjar's head shows its short, soft bill, wide gape and the stiff rictal bristles. The large eye is typical of a nocturnal bird.

SOME SPECIALISED BILLS

The Trumpeter Hornbill has a hollow casque on its bill for amplifying sound.

Insectivorous birds have short, slender bills.

Parrots' powerful bills are designed for cracking large, hard-shelled seeds and extracting the kernels.

Many insectivorous birds have long, curved bills for probing into soft ground.

Kingfishers have sharp, dagger-like bills for catching and holding fish.

A skimmer uses its longer lower mandible to plough through surface-water while flying. On contact with a fish the bill snaps shut.

The huge, hooked bill of a large vulture is a tool for tearing the tough hide of animals killed by four-legged predators.

The slender, curved bill of sunbirds, coupled with their long tongues, enables them to probe deep into flowers to reach the nectar.

Short, stout bills are for crushing seeds.

Rollers feed on large grasshoppers, beetles, scorpions, lizards and small frogs.

Many ocean birds have external, tubular nostrils through which excess sea salt is expelled.

The huge Saddle-billed Stork has an equally large and colourful bill with a yellow 'saddle' which gives this bird its name.

The Great White Pelican has an extendible pouch below its bill that is used as a scoop for catching fish.

The African Spoonbill moves its partially open bill through the water in a sideways, sweeping motion to catch small aquatic creatures.

The Lesser Moorhen, in common with many of its relatives, has a colourful 'frontal shield' on its forehead.

The Avocet uses its recurved bill to sweep the water's surface for small organisms.

The powerful hooked bills of raptors are used for tearing the flesh of their prey.

FEATHER STRUCTURE AND ARRANGEMENT

A feather is made up of a main shaft, from which vanes project. Each vane has barbs and interlocking barbules; when the barbules become unlocked the bird relocks them by drawing them through its bill while preening. The body of a bird is covered with an underlying layer of soft down feathers that have no interlocking barbules, and they in turn are covered by contour feathers that cover all regions except the beak and the scaled parts of the legs and feet. This double feather layer serves to both insulate and streamline the body, to keep it waterproof and to protect the skin from abrasive wind-borne particles.

The main feathers of the wing are the flight feathers, made up of:

1. outer primary feathers, attached to the 'hand'
2. secondary feathers, attached to the 'forearm'
3. tertiary feathers, attached to the humerus or 'upper arm'
4. The small bastard wing or alula

THE UPPER WING OF A BIRD

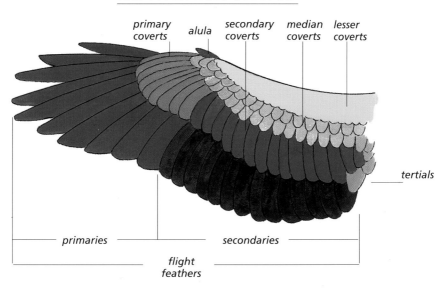

The shape of a bird's wing varies: it is short and rounded in birds that fly little, or long and tapering in fast-flying birds. The primary feathers are the most important in a bird's wing and can be likened to the fingers of a human hand. Most birds have nine primary feathers, but some have as many as 12. Between the primary feathers and the bird's body are the secondary feathers, and these can number from 10 to 12 in passerines or as many as 32 in the larger albatrosses. The bases of these major wing feathers, where they join the bone within the wing, are covered by overlaying contour feathers called 'coverts'. The base of the primary feathers are covered by the primary coverts, the secondaries by the secondary coverts and so on, each successive row of coverts getting smaller than the preceding one to produce a smooth wing surface.

Above left: *A Cattle Egret displaying its nuptial plumes plus red bill and leg colouring.*
Above middle left: *The head crest of a Red-eyed Bulbul can be erected at will.*
Above middle right: *The Crowned Eagle with raised crest is an intimidating sight.*
Above right: *The tail of an incubating male Paradise Flycatcher almost negates the purpose of its inconspicuous nest.*

P. Steyn

Above: *The Long-crested Eagle is the most easily recognised large raptor; note its wide, yellow gape.*

The flight feathers (remiges) and tail feathers (rectrices) are stiffened to provide a strong, smooth surface that can be manipulated by the bird for maximum flight efficiency. Looking at a bird's upper wing surface, one sees that the bases of the primaries are covered by contour feathers, called primary coverts, while the bases of the secondaries are similarly covered by the secondary coverts. Further forward, the bases of these coverts are covered in turn by the median coverts, then the lesser coverts, and finally the small marginal coverts on the leading edge of the wing. A similar arrangement is seen on the underwing. This succession of contour feathers provides the wing with a smooth surface and an unimpeded air-flow. The alula consists of small quill feathers attached to the base of the first primary. They prevent the wing from stalling at slow flying speeds.

MOULTING

All birds moult their feathers once a year, usually after breeding: the post-nuptial moult. The moulting process is normally gradual, especially in the wing feathers, where opposing feathers in each wing are shed simultaneously. In some ducks and geese the flight feathers are all shed simultaneously, rendering the birds flightless for several weeks. For safety in these circumstances the birds retreat to moult on large waters where they remain until they are able to fly again.

G. Lockwood

This Fork-tailed Drongo is regrowing its outer tail feathers following its moult.

20 birds by colour

Many bird species have specialised or ornate feathers that may be used in display, particularly in courtship. Such feathers may have extended shafts, as seen in the long tails of male widows, whydahs and the Paradise Flycatcher. Others have extendible head crests, as seen in mousebirds, louries or the Long-crested Eagle, while many herons and egrets develop filamentous plumes on their heads, breasts or backs during the breeding season.

Below: *When birds preen each other, like these White-faced Ducks, it is called 'allopreening', a mutual comfort-action.*

PREENING

Because a bird's feathers are so important they are given regular care and maintenance by preening. Dirty or disarranged feathers are cleaned or rearranged mostly by being pulled through the bird's bill, but its feet are also used for certain functions, such as scratching to loosen dust, old feather particles and parasitic mites. Many birds have a gland on their rump near the base of the tail, which secretes oil when the bill or head rubs on it. The oil is then distributed over the feather surfaces, especially the flight feathers, and probably serves to condition them.

In addition to these activities, birds will also bathe in water or in dust. Even gulls that spend much time in seawater fly to freshwater ponds or lagoons to bathe and preen.

A male Cape Sparrow preening its shoulder.

G. Lockwood

COLOUR IN FEATHERS

Humans are mainly attracted to colourful birds and pay much less attention to the plainly coloured ones, or LBJs (little brown jobs) as they are called. However, within the bird's world, dull colours are as important and as functional as bright ones, and may make the difference between the survival or extinction of a species.

In species with sexually different plumages (sexual dimorphism) the difference is often only marked for a short duration. The male Red Bishop, for example, wears its bright plumage only during the breeding season, after which it assumes a drab plumage similar to the female's.

Bright colours or bold markings in a bird serve to advertise the individual's presence in different situations, aid species or mate recognition, and are functional in territorial display and courtship. The male Red Bishop patrols the region surrounding the females and their nests in regular territorial flights or by perching conspicuously, always with

Above left: *A male Red Bishop in full display.*
Above right: *A male Red Bishop moulting into breeding plumage.*
Right and below right: *An Orange-throated Longclaw at its nest in the grass. Note how the colour of its throat matches that of its chick's gape in the nest behind it.*

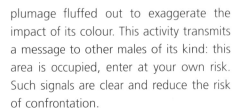

plumage fluffed out to exaggerate the impact of its colour. This activity transmits a message to other males of its kind: this area is occupied, enter at your own risk. Such signals are clear and reduce the risk of confrontation.

The fact that birds, especially when defending a territory, react strongly to colour has been well demonstrated. In an experiment carried out in Europe, a stuffed robin was placed in the territory of a resident robin. The territorial bird immediately attacked the stuffed bird so violently and persistently that it literally knocked the stuffing out of it. The resident robin was reacting to the orange breast of the stuffed bird.

The Masked Weaver male assuming the brightest or boldest breeding plumage in spring and building the first acceptable nest on which to display both his colours and his handiwork is likely to be the most successful in attracting females.

The breast-bands on birds, often black, not only serve as clear territorial signals but may also function as recognition features and as an aid when feeding their young. When the well-known Cattle Egret has nestlings, its bill assumes a bright orange-red colour, and the sight of this causes the chicks to open their bills and beg for food. Experiments have shown that when artificial bills of different colours are shown to the chicks they do not respond until a 'bill' of the correct colour is used. The Orange-throated Longclaw has a bright orange-red throat surrounded by a black border, which is at its most brilliant during breeding. The nestlings of this species have identical orange-red mouth interiors. When the parent bird comes to the nest with food the chicks, on seeing the brightly coloured throat, are stimulated into opening their gapes to receive the food. The parent, in turn, on seeing the chicks' bright gapes is stimulated into delivering the meal. These reactions are inbred and involve no thought process on the part of either parent or chick. One assumes that if the longclaw's throat were to be painted another colour, then the chicks would not be fed.

A Cattle Egret nestling will only accept food presented by the orange bill of its parents (left). When offered a bill of another colour the chick shows no interest (right).

We have discussed the conspicuous breeding plumages of the male Red Bishop and the Masked Weaver, but why do the females remain comparatively dull at this time? The answer lies in their need to be inconspicuous. The females take no part in territorial defence and do not display but go about the job of incubating their eggs and raising their young; a time when the avoidance of predators has its advantages.

Many species maintain dull colouring in both sexes at all times, especially warblers and others that prefer a secretive way of life in their chosen reed or thicket habitats.

Cryptic colours, by which certain birds, their nests, eggs and young blend with their surroundings, demonstrate well the art of camouflage. Nightjars have the most cryptic plumage, while among plovers and other ground nesters both eggs and young are remarkably well camouflaged to avoid detection.

CONCEALING THE COLOURS

Birds that wear vivid plumage at all times, such as rollers, bee-eaters, barbets and hornbills, are invariably hole nesters. Once inside their nest chamber they are not visible to predators; even their eggs are conspicuously white.

Both the newly hatched chick and egg of the ground-nesting Crowned Plover are cryptically coloured.

THE FLYING BIRD

The sight of a bird flapping through the air is such an everyday experience that it is seldom given a second thought. However, getting into a mere flap gets no-one anywhere, let alone the bird. The flapping wing may get the bird into the air vertically but it needs more than this to get it moving. Propulsion is achieved by the bird lifting its wings and thrusting them downward and backward in an oar-like movement. It is difficult for us to see the backward thrust unless shown in slow-action photography.

Heavy-bodied birds with their greater wing-loading, such as guineafowl, need to flap vigorously to remain airborne; otherwise, like vultures, eagles and storks, they must seek less exhausting ways of remaining aloft. These soaring birds do so by seeking rising warm air. On sunny days, ploughed fields, buildings and warm, sheltered valleys cause bubbles

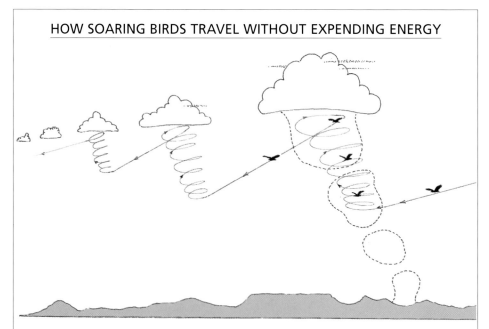

HOW SOARING BIRDS TRAVEL WITHOUT EXPENDING ENERGY

Warm, moist air, heated by the sun, accumulates in valleys, over towns and in rocky places. When the air becomes warmer than its surroundings it breaks away to rise in large 'bubbles' or warm columns called thermals. (In Africa, thermals are often visible as 'dust devils'). As the thermal reaches cooler altitudes, the moisture within it condenses and forms a cumulus cloud which continues to grow as more heat and moisture reaches it. Large birds such as storks, eagles and buzzards seek these thermals and circle within them to gain height without needing to flap their wings. Once the bird has reached the base of the cumulus cloud, usually between 1 000 and 2 000 m above ground, it sets course again and glides, gradually losing height as it goes, until it encounters the next thermal and regains the height lost in the glide. During a typical sunny day, a soaring bird can travel cross-country for at least seven hours in this way with the minimum exertion.

of warm air to rise. Since they are warmer than the surrounding air, these bubbles rise quickly, sometimes to a great height. By circling in these warm air bubbles or thermals, large birds are able not only to gain height without flapping their wings but to travel cross-country.

Because gravity is at all times trying to pull the bird back to earth, the use of a thermal to gain height is akin to a person walking slowly down an ascending escalator; the escalator will get you to the top although you have been walking down.

To remain airborne when gliding a bird must maintain a certain minimum airspeed. The heavier the bird, the faster its airspeed when gliding. Should its airspeed fall below the minimum, its wings will stall and the bird will fall unless it flaps its wings. If, say, a bird's normal gliding speed, with no wing-flapping, is 20 kilometres an hour (km/h) in relation to the air, and if it is facing into a wind blowing at 20 km/h, then the bird will remain motionless in relation to the ground. If the wind increased to 30 km/h the bird would move backward at 10 km/h in relation to the ground, but the airspeed over its wings would remain at 20 km/h. When a Black-breasted Snake Eagle or a Black-shouldered Kite is seen to hover on motionless wings it has merely adjusted its forward speed to that of the approaching wind.

BIRD MIGRATION

Migrations may be long-distance, as seen in the millions of birds that arrive in Africa from Europe and the Arctic Circle every year in our early summer, or they may be within Africa, the so-called intra-Africa migrants. Another form of local migration is a comparatively short-distance, altitudinal one in which many birds move annually at the onset of the cold season from high ground to lower, coastal regions.

Birds that migrate into Africa from the northern hemisphere (the Palaearctic region) do so at the onset of the northern winter. At this time temperatures, especially within the Arctic Circle, drop to well below freezing. With waters frozen over and the land deep in snow there is little food for birds. The great southward movement to warmer, food-rich regions involves countless millions of birds of every description, large and small. This migration takes place over a wide front and, while millions move into Africa, others move into India, China and even Australia. At the same time a similar movement occurs between North America and South America in the great worldwide trek for survival.

In Africa, birds arrive in September-October and return north again in March-April, just before the onset of our winter. As they arrive in the northern regions some weeks later, the ice and snow of the north are starting to thaw. Suddenly there is a great hatching of flies, mosquitoes and many other insects, in addition to the birth of countless small mammals. An inhospitable land becomes the land of plenty for a few short summer months. In these ideal conditions birds breed and feed their young; smaller birds take advantage of the insect glut or the spawning fish, while raptors exploit newly born rodents and other birds.

How do birds find their way?

Navigation for day-flying migrants is based on inherent instinct and a visual memory of well-used routes. Many smaller birds navigate by observing the position of the sun. There are three major migratory routes into Africa. In the first and most used route, the birds converge on the Bosporus in the eastern Mediterranean and continue south through Turkey and Israel into Egypt, so avoiding a lengthy sea crossing. The second route converges on Gibraltar, where the birds have a short sea crossing into Morocco. The third and least used route carries them down Italy and to various Mediterranean islands. Although it involves crossing both sea and the Sahara Desert, this route is nevertheless preferred by certain species.

Once in Africa, the eastern migrants follow the Nile River and physical features of the land, such as mountain ranges and the African lakes of the Rift Valley, before finally fanning out to their various eventual destinations. In the west, those from the Gibraltar crossing tend to follow the West African coastline before entering the tropics.

Perhaps the most remarkable long-distance migrants are the warblers. These diminutive birds travel some 12 000 km, flying at night and navigating by the stars.

PRINCIPAL MIGRATION ROUTES BETWEEN EUROPE AND AFRICA

Most birds on migration avoid lengthy ocean crossings whenever possible. The map shows the main migration routes between the Palearctic region (Europe, Scandinavia and Western Russia) and Africa. The popular Bosporus and Gibraltar routes avoid lengthy sea and desert crossings, yet many small birds do take a direct route across the Mediterranean and the Sahara Desert.

A Garden Warbler, typical of the many small Palearctic migrants that arrive in southern Africa in our summer.

Although they rest by day there is little opportunity for feeding; instead they rely on their own fat reserves, often arriving in southern Africa having lost a third of their original body weight. Shorebirds and seabirds tend to follow coastlines or rivers and lakes. They fly fast and non-stop day and night; then, on sighting a convenient shoreline or estuary, may spend several days feeding before continuing their journey.

How long do birds spend migrating?

It is difficult to know when many birds leave on migration, or exactly when they arrive, but bird ringing has provided some answers. The majority of birds seem to take about six weeks for the journey, depending on their method of travel and weather conditions *en route*. The record holder is a European Swallow that, along with many others, was ringed and released in Germiston, South Africa, and recaptured in Moscow, Russia, 32 days later.

G. Lockwood

BIRD RINGING

Bird ringing is a research tool used by trained members of bird clubs to determine bird movements, longevity and certain other aspects of their lives. The birds are caught in very fine 'mist nets' that capture them without injury. Each bird's leg is then fitted with a small, lightweight metal ring carrying a distinct number and the address of the national bird-ringing unit that issued the ring. All the details of the bird are recorded before it is released so that, when it is eventually recovered, dead or alive, its age and the distance it has travelled in the interim can be ascertained.

A mist net being used to catch birds near a water reservoir.

METHODS OF FEEDING

Birds as a whole feed on almost anything that lives on this earth, be it animal or vegetable. The ways in which many birds go about obtaining their food, however, is fascinating and often unique.

Most herons and egrets stalk their fish with stealth and great patience, but the Black Egret makes fish-spotting easier by mantling its wings to cut out surface reflection. The Green-backed Heron has shown a remarkable instance of tool usage by a bird. This heron

A Black Egret, with its wings mantled, has a quick look around between bouts of fishing.

The Squacco Heron feeds on small fishes and insects, hunting them with stealth.

sometimes uses 'bait' to attract fish within reach of its bill. It will seize a small insect or spider and place it on the water, watching carefully for a fish to rise. If the 'bait' should begin to float away, the heron will replace it within reach until an unsuspecting fish responds.

Both Eastern White and Pink-backed Pelicans will sometimes indulge in co-operative fishing, a dozen or more birds herding a fish shoal into the shallows while swimming in close formation and repeatedly plunging their bills in unison. This is followed by a feeding frenzy, each bird plunging and replunging its bill into the fish shoal and scooping them up in its net-like pouch.

A flock of Eastern White Pelicans herding a shoal of fish.

At sea, especially, fish hunting also takes place from the air. This is well demonstrated by the Cape Gannet and its tropical cousins, the boobies. Both gannets and boobies plunge-dive from a height of 20-30 metres to catch fish, while Brown- and Red-footed Boobies pursue and overtake flying fish, which are often disturbed by the bows of a moving ship. A gannet's breast is protected by a number of air sacs beneath the skin that cushion its impact with the water when plunge-diving.

Wilson's, Red-necked and Grey Phalaropes are rare visitors to our shores, and can be described as long-legged sandpipers that spend many months of the year feeding at sea. Their unique method of feeding has the bird swimming rapidly in a tight circle that creates a miniature whirlpool. The resultant vortex action of the water brings small insects and plankton towards the surface where they are snapped up by the phalarope.

The aerial pirates of the sea are undoubtedly skuas and frigatebirds. Skuas are dark brown, gull-like seabirds from the cooler oceans, that obtain their fish by chasing and harrying other seabirds to make them disgorge. Frigatebirds are huge, long-winged,

The magnificent Frigatebird, a pirate of the tropical seas.

fork-tailed, blackish birds that perform much the same action in the tropics. Even the larger species, with a two-metre wingspan, are highly manoeuvrable in flight. Although frigatebirds feed at sea they seldom enter the water.

The African Skimmer's bill has an elongated lower mandible. The bird flies just above the surface of the water with its lower mandible immersed, skimming the surface in a sort of blind hit-and-miss forage. On striking a small fish, the jaw is snapped shut and the prey is swallowed, either in flight or after the bird settles.

Inland birds are not without their unique feeding habits. Woodpeckers seek the grubs of ants, termites and woodboring beetles, which are often unseen, deep in their feeding tunnels within trees. To reach them, woodpeckers are equipped with either a sticky or a barbed tongue. The very long, extensible tongue is inserted deep into the grub's tunnel to locate and extract the prey.

Some of the most interesting feeding behaviour is seen in our birds of prey. The Bearded Vulture is partial to bones and bone marrow. When the bones are too large to be swallowed they are taken into the air in the bird's feet and dropped from a height onto rocks to break them. Usually the vulture has a favourite dropping area, and it may require several drops to shatter large bones. Another vulture with a strange diet is the Palm-nut Vulture. Fairly catholic in its tastes, the Palm-nut Vulture will eat a variety of fruit and small animals in addition to stranded fish and carrion found on the sea and river shores. But its name derives from its habit of feeding on the fruits of raffia palms, and it seldom moves far from these trees.

Another example of an odd diet for a large bird is that of the Steppe Eagle, a summer visitor from Eastern Europe and Asia. The Steppe Eagle is related to our resident Tawny Eagle, but is somewhat larger. While in Africa, the preferred diet

A Cardinal Woodpecker using its long, barbed tongue to extract a wood borer beetle grub from its burrow deep in a tree.

A Gymnogene investigating the interior of a wood-pecker's nest-hole in a tree.

of these eagles is termite alates, commonly called 'flying ants'. To collect them, the eagles congregate at the point where the termites emerge. They are seldom alone. Tawny Eagles, Lesser Spotted Eagles and even Bateleurs will join in the feast.

The Gymnogene forages for lizards, amphibians, small mammals, insects, young birds and birds' eggs. This large-winged hawk has long legs that are able to bend in three directions from the tarsal joint. It raids the nests of weavers, swallows, swifts, woodpeckers and others, hanging on with one foot while the other is inserted into the nest of its victim. Not unnaturally the Gymnogene is unpopular among small birds, which will mob it whenever they have the chance.

Small owls prey on insects, birds and small rodents, while large owls obviously feed on larger prey. What is surprising is that many owls prey on other owls. The Giant Eagle Owl will kill others as large as the Spotted Eagle Owl. In one reported observation, a Giant Eagle Owl was found feeding on a Pel's Fishing Owl, a bird equal in size to its predator.

DISPLAY IN COURTSHIP, AGGRESSION AND FEAR

As discussed under '*Colour in Feathers*,' birds will display themselves to conspecifics (others of the same species) in defence of their territory through plumage colours or patterns. However, many other forms of display are used in courtship and pair bonding. These include the use of plumage colours, plumage manipulations, posturing or a combination of these and others. Many displays are highly ritualised and it is often difficult to detect the narrow margin between courtship and aggressive displays. A posture that can commonly be seen in the garden is that adopted during the breeding season by the Olive Thrush. The male thrush, when courting a female, will strut about with its wings drooped and its fanned tail scraping the ground. However, should another male approach too closely it will use the same posture to drive it away. Another easily seen courtship display is that used by many ducks, in which the male will swim towards the

W. Tarboton

The conspicuous territorial display of the Long-tailed Widow.

female while bobbing its head. In some species both sexes bob or shake their heads as a form of pair bonding (the strengthening of their relationship). Egyptian Geese pairs form long-term relationships and, should the pairs become temporarily separated, the return of the missing individual involves a noisy and highly ritualised pair bonding. The two geese approach each other with out-stretched necks and much loud calling, and then rub their necks together.

In that colourful garden bird, the Bokmakierie, courtship involves both sexes facing each other on the ground and shuffling around in a circle, alternatively bowing to the ground and 'sky-pointing' with their bills while making hardly discernible sounds.

Some bustards and korhaans are noted for their extravagant displays during courtship, and the Kori Bustard is no exception. The male struts with its head thrown back and breast feathers splayed outward to expose the white under-feathers, while the tail is thrown upward and forward to display the white feathers beneath. These and similar plumage transformations are used in several large species. The only time that the brick-red crest of the male Red-crested Korhaan is exposed is during its courtship display. The male circles around the female in a sort of hop-and-jump action while making soft calls.

Cranes in courtship indulge in elegant dances, each member of the pair leaping and twisting around with wings out-spread, uttering bugling calls. Single birds within a flock can be seen doing this silently from time to time, probably in an attempt to stimulate others to reciprocate.

Egyptian Geese engaged in a greeting ritual.

An Olive Thrush displaying.

W. Tarboton

The 'bubble display' of the male Maccoa Duck.

Above: *As its ground nest is approached by a potential predator, a Crowned Plover assumes an aggressive posture with its wings fully extended and calling loudly.*
Above right: *When the aggressor continues to approach the nest, the plover becomes undecided between aggression and retreat, and so directs its aggression in a neutral direction while still calling.*
Right: *As a final strategy, the plover feigns injury, running away in the 'broken-wing' posture to encourage the predator to follow it and so move away from the nest.*

In mild aggression, such as during territorial or feeding encounters, birds will spread their wings and those with head-crests will raise them, while many others will merely raise their head feathers or their body contour feathers or both. These actions serve to intimidate the opposition by making the bird appear larger.

With many plovers, and ducks too, the incubating bird will flush from the nest at the last moment in the face of disturbance, and flop away with one wing outstretched as though disabled – a display termed 'injury feigning'. It serves to draw the intruder away from the nest in the hope of catching the apparently injured bird. In this case the displaying bird stays just ahead of its pursuer and flies off at the last moment, only to return to its eggs when the danger has passed.

THE NESTS THEY BUILD

Birds build nests primarily as a place in which to lay their eggs and to raise their young, but many small birds build them for roosting purposes outside the breeding season. The nests chosen as roosts are usually of the domed type, where many individuals may crowd together for shared bodily warmth.

The term 'nest' brings to mind an intricate construction, as is certainly made by numerous birds, but in most terrestrial species the eggs are laid on the bare ground, or at best in a shallow depression scraped out by the bird's feet. Coursers, pratincoles, dikkops, plovers, bustards and nightjars all lay their clutches on open ground. In many cases ground nesters will lay their eggs close to some obstacle, such as a stone, a dried mammal dropping or a fallen branch, a disruptive ploy that serves to render both the eggs and the incubating bird less obvious to potential predators. Others, such as the African Black Oystercatcher which lays its eggs on the seashore, do so among dried seaweed at the high tide mark, while the White-fronted Sand Plover and others may allow the sand to almost obscure the eggs.

Perhaps the most widely used nest type is the conventional cup-shaped nest of thrushes, robins, wagtails, flycatchers, shrikes and many others. The basic materials of these nests are grasses, rootlets, bark strips, leaves and hair, often with a softer lining. In contrast, the Olive Thrush and others line the nest with mud. Many flycatchers and members of the shrike family decorate the outside of the nest with lichens and then bind it with spider web for added strength.

Largest of the cup-shaped nests are those of eagles and some storks. Eagles use dry sticks to build the nest, adding to it in successive years until it may become three to four metres in height. Most eagles practise a form of nest hygiene by lining the bowl of the nest daily with fresh green leaves.

Some birds gather small feathers to line their nests, especially sparrows and others that construct an enclosed nest. Many ducks actually pluck soft down from their own breasts to create a thick, warm layer for the eggs. Eiderdown comes from the breast of the female Eider Duck of the northern hemisphere, and is collected commercially in Iceland.

Weaver nests are as variable as the materials used to build them. The Spectacled Weaver constructs a long tunnel entrance to its nest, which may serve to deter predators; the Thick-billed Weaver's nest is made of the finest materials; and the Red-headed Weaver builds a

1.

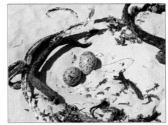

2.

3.

W. Tarboton

4.

G. Lockwood

1. *A male Masked Weaver building its nest.*
2. *The African Black Oystercatcher, a ground-nester on our coastline, lays its eggs among dried kelp at the high tide mark as a disruptive ploy.*
3. *A female Chin-spot Batis on its small, cup-shaped nest.*
4. *A male Thick-billed Weaver at its nest of fine grasses and tendrils.*

nest of pliable, hairy twigs. The hairy covering of the twigs causes them to lock firmly together but, since the twigs are brown in colour, the nest appears to be old from the outset. Sociable Weavers, a species from the drier western regions, carry gregariousness to the extreme. Their massive nest structures, with 50 or more separate nest chambers, are added to constantly and may eventually break under their own weight.

The most intricate ball-type nests are those of Cape and Grey Penduline Tits. Their nests are soft, oval balls of tightly felted plant and animal wool and spider webs. The entrance is a protruding spout near to the top on one side, but immediately below it there is a false entrance. When the bird leaves the nest it stands on the rim of the false entrance and closes the real entrance by pushing upwards with its head. On returning it stands on the rim of the false entrance and pulls the real entrance open with its beak or foot, closing it again once it has entered.

The communal nest of Sociable Weavers may reach massive dimensions.

P. Steyn

Left: *The Cape Penduline Tit's remarkable nest of plant down and animal fur showing both the entrance spout and the false entrance below it.*
Below left: *The White-throated Swallow, in common with many other swallows, builds a bowl of mud pellets and grass which is attached to a rock or wall.*
Below: *A Lanner Falcon attending its chicks in a Martial Eagle's nest.*

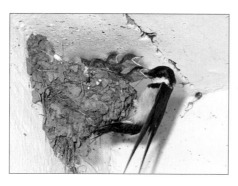

Swallows build nests of mud gathered from puddles. Their nests may be cup-shaped or enclosed, and are fastened firmly under a rock, a branch or a building overhang. The inverted retort-shaped mud nests of striped swallows and others are similar to the nests used by burrow nesters and hole nesters. Some swallows and their relatives, the martins, nest in deep burrows in riverbanks or road cuttings, the nest chambers being at the end of a half-metre tunnel.

Falcons, kestrels and owls make no nest at all. They either lay their eggs on a rock ledge or, as often happens, in the disused nest of another raptor, adding no extra material to the chosen site.

WHAT DO I NEED TO GO BIRDING?

The answer is 'very little'. The most expensive and necessary piece of equipment is a pair of binoculars. You can't look at distant or small birds without them. Today the choice of makes and models is so wide that it really depends on how much you are prepared to spend. Although the upper limits are in the thousands, there are many very usable binoculars in the R500 to R1 000 price range. Spend as much as you can afford – it will be a worthwhile investment. When choosing binoculars, there are a few golden rules to bear in mind. Cheap binoculars have poor lenses that may damage your eyes and the lenses themselves are glued into place. If the binoculars receive a knock, the lenses are likely to fall out of alignment. Binoculars should feel comfortable in the hands and should not be so heavy that you cannot hold them steady. They should also feel light and comfortable when hanging around your neck, otherwise you may discover that a few hours of birding can literally become a pain in the neck! If you wear spectacles, get binoculars that have roll-back rubber eyepieces.

For birdwatching I recommend roof-prism binoculars rather than barrel-type binoculars because they are more compact and easier to hold (see illustrations). The best binoculars for birdwatching are within the range of 7,5 x 30, 8 x 35 and 10 x 40-50. The first number is the magnification, which means that 8 x binoculars will enlarge the bird eight times. The second number is the millimetre diameter of the large front lens. Thus in 8 x 35 binoculars the front lenses each have a diameter of 35 mm. The larger the diameter of the front lenses the wider the field of view and the brighter the image, because a wide lens gathers more light. Image brightness is particularly important when viewing birds in poor light, and a wide field of view facilitates locating the bird, especially in flight, through the binoculars. My personal preference is 10 x 40 or 10 x 50 roof-prism binoculars.

Don't hurry your purchase of binoculars. Examine and handle many before you finally decide. First be sure that the lenses are adjusted to your eyes; the salesperson will show you how to do this. Test the binoculars by going to the shop door and focusing on some object at a distance. The image must be sharp and clear without any colour aberration. Should the image be surrounded by a colour outline, the lenses are inferior and possibly harmful to your eyes.

Barrel type binoculars.

Roof-prism binoculars.

Compact roof-prism binoculars, suitable for the pocket or handbag, are popular and particularly useful when travelling. They are very small and usually come in 8 x 20, 10 x 22 or thereabouts. However, as the front lenses are small, their light gathering capability is low and the field of view is very narrow, but as a second pair for travel or emergencies they are handy.

While I do not recommend that you buy a telescope initially, there will probably come a time that you feel the need. This is especially true when looking at distant shorebirds. The guidelines for purchasing a scope are much the same as for binoculars, but of course one also needs a tripod.

The second thing you need when birdwatching is a bird book, better known as a fieldguide. It is necessary to have a fieldguide that illustrates the birds clearly, describes each bird and provides a map of its distribution. The best of these books are fairly small and easy to carry. The type of fieldguide you choose will depend on the layout and style of illustration that most appeals to you. Some fieldguides use photographs to illustrate the birds while others use paintings. Even when good photographs are used there are shortcomings, in that each bird is usually illustrated by only one picture. Also, with some of the rarer, difficult-to-photograph species, the author often needs to rely on second-rate photographs or resort to a painting.

The advantage of hand-painted illustrations is that there is no limit to the number of pictures that can be used for each bird. Species that have different adult and immature plumages, and those that have plumage variations, can all be shown in addition to flight pictures. In my own fieldguide, *Newman's Birds of Southern Africa*, it has been possible in some instances to show six or more illustrations of one species.

Another advantage of hand-painted illustrations is that birds can be consistently depicted in their most characteristic attitudes and with their most useful field features highlighted, something not usually possible in photographs.

So much for expenses. The next and final piece of equipment you should arm yourself with is a small notebook and a pencil or ballpoint pen. Cultivate the habit of making notes of the birds you have seen, particularly when you are not sure what you've spotted. A simple sketch, no matter how crude, with notes about beak shape, leg colour, habitat, etc. will prove essential when you page through your fieldguide that evening trying to identify 'the one that got away' or 'the bird that isn't in Newman's book'.

I cannot over-emphasise the advantage of going into the field with helpful, more experienced birders; it's the quickest way to learn. Bird clubs, with their weekend and day outings, provide this essential service. So, if there's a club near you, why not go along? You'll also find that your local bird club offers evening lectures about birds by their more experienced members, usually accompanied by slides or films, and may provide a quarterly coloured bird magazine and a newsletter about forthcoming club activities.

WHERE TO LOOK FOR BIRDS

The best place to begin looking for birds is in your own garden or local park. You are likely to find at least 20 species with which to familiarise yourself, and they provide a good starting point for searches farther afield. Away from the garden, birds can be found almost anywhere. You may be surprised to know that the Karoo is rich in birds. Even deserts have their special bird inhabitants. Some regions certainly have a richer avifauna than others, and it is wise to become familiar with their locations.

A typical wetland with a flock of White-winged Terns.

Wetlands

This name is applied to a wide variety of inland waterways and other moist situations. Unspoilt wetlands are highly productive for the birder and I recommend them as a very good habitat in which to enjoy your early bird-watching. The birds in a wetland are, for the most part, fairly large, easy to see and reasonably easily identified. Of course, in summer, there are often a number of little grey shorebirds and they may initially prove difficult to correctly identify; leave them for later, when you have gained more experience.

Most waterbirds belong to the non-passerine group, so many will have long legs or long beaks, even striking plumages. In wetlands you may discover various herons, ibises, ducks and geese, flamingoes, storks and others that may be quite new to you. Having started at a productive wetland you may come away having identified 10 or more new birds, and that gives great confidence.

Near the coast, the best wetlands are river estuaries, backwaters and lagoons. Inland farm dams or marshes can be very productive, with sewage disposal pans top of the waterbird list. Bird clubs have prearranged access to many such locations. Many wetlands, especially within municipal boundaries or nature reserves, have hides that make it possible to sit and watch the birds without them seeing you. Otherwise it's a good idea to watch them from a car. Remember that most birds are wary of human beings but are tolerant of cars.

Bushveld

This is a term sometimes applied loosely to any indigenous wooded region, whether the vegetation be bushes, trees or a mixture of both. Whatever its composition it is likely to be a very productive bird habitat. Bushveld covers vast areas of the land both within reserves and without, and it falls into the two broad categories of thornveld and broad-leaved woodland.

Thornveld is a habitat of predominantly thorn bushes, and is highly attractive to many birds, both those that feed in the thorny canopies and on the ground. In bushveld you should watch the ground for francolins, guineafowls, sandgrouse, larks and waxbills. Check the lower stratum of the bushes for tchagra shrikes, boubous and prinias, and within the canopies for bush shrikes, eremomelas and other warblers. At higher levels watch for flycatchers, drongos, starlings, weavers, barbets and sunbirds, while some taller trees may harbour woodpeckers and birds of prey.

Broad-leaved woodland, in which the grassy understorey is fairly open and the trees are well spaced, supports a number of canopy-feeding birds. These can include birds of prey, flycatchers, bush shrikes, woodpeckers and tits. The main difference between this and other habitats is that bird inhabitants of woodland normally occur in mixed groups called 'bird parties'. One may walk for, say, 10 minutes without seeing birds; then, suddenly, one encounters a bird party and is hard put to record them all before they have passed on.

Riverine bush or forest

Also called riparian woodland or forest. As its name indicates this is the well-treed woodland of many river banks where, better watered than the surrounding bush, the trees tend to be larger and evergreen. It is invariably good for birds of all kinds, including louries, flycatchers, cuckooshrikes, birds of prey and, during summer, cuckoos and kingfishers.

Grasslands

Don't ignore grasslands; they harbour numerous interesting birds, from larks, pipits, widows, korhaans and cisticolas to francolins and cranes. Grasslands are particularly active during summer when many of the widows and bishops adopt their colourful breeding plumages, and others are making their presence known by calling.

Evergreen forests

Evergreen forests include a great variety of indigenous trees and are found in regions of good rainfall, from the kloofs of the Drakensberg escarpment eastward to the coastal regions and south to the Eastern Cape. These beautiful forests are home to a variety of special birds. The forest robins and thrushes, the Emerald Cuckoo, Knysna Lourie and Crowned Eagle are all there for the finding, but be warned that locating them is no easy task. They can certainly be heard as they call from high in the forest canopies, but seeing them calls for great patience, much neck-stretching and perseverance.

WHEN TO LOOK FOR BIRDS

The majority of birds are with us all year round, but a few are seasonal migrants that arrive here in our spring and depart again in late summer. Birds generally are most active during the morning, from dawn until about 10h30, and in the evening, from about 16h30 till last light. During the middle of the day they tend to rest, or at least be less active, especially in hot weather. Exceptions are the high-flying eagles and vultures, but even these are most active during the first half of the day. Nocturnal birds – owls, nightjars and dikkops – are most active between dusk and midnight, and longer when the moon is bright. Nightjars do much of their feeding during the first few hours of darkness and can often be seen flying at dusk.

When reading about a bird in your fieldguide, check whether it is a resident or migrant. If the latter, it is unlikely to be seen between mid-April and mid-September.

HOW TO LOOK AT BIRDS

When looking at an unfamiliar bird, make a habit of mentally noting its important features so that you will remember them once it has flown. The following simple system should prove helpful. There are six stages that, after a little practice, will be remembered subconsciously:

1. Note the bird's approximate size.
2. Check its beak.
3. Check its legs.
4. Note its body markings or colours.
5. Note the habitat it is in.
6. Note what it is doing.

1. What was its size?

A good way to memorise a bird's size is to compare it with three common birds that you know. Is it smaller or larger than a sparrow (mossie)? If larger, is it smaller or larger than a city pigeon? If larger, is the bird smaller or larger than a guineafowl? Try to establish this in your mind while you are looking at the bird.

Tiny coloured birds on the edge of the track are waxbills or finches.

2. Beak shape and colour

This is important. The beak may be long and slender as in some shorebirds. It may be curved downward like that of a bee-eater or sunbird, or curved upward as in the Avocet. It may be short and stout as seen in the seed-eating sparrows, weavers and canaries, or hooked as in birds of prey and parrots. Some birds have coloured beaks. These points need to be memorised or noted.

3. Leg length and colour

Legs are also important identity clues. Are the bird's legs of 'normal' length in proportion to its body size, as seen for example in sparrows or thrushes? The legs may be long, even very long, as in many waterbirds, or very short, as seen in swallows and swifts. If they are long, what colour are they?

4. Plumage colours and markings

The colours or plumage markings that first strike you should be memorised. Note whether the bird has colour on its head, breast, tail or wings, or if it has any bold markings, such as a white wing-bar or black band across its breast. These are important clues for identification.

5. What habitat was it in?

The habitat in which you see the bird is also an important clue to its identity, as certain look-alikes are found in totally different habitats.

6. What was the bird doing?

The bird's behaviour is another important clue to its identity. It might be swimming, wading, flying or merely walking. If the bird is in a tree, then what is it doing in the tree? It could be feeding in the outer leaves of the canopy (warbler) or perched on top of the tree (flycatcher, shrike or drongo) or on one side of the tree (roller or kingfisher). The bird could be pecking at the tree trunk or a branch (woodpecker or barbet).

These six points will help you to decide on the bird's identity (ID) when reading fieldguide descriptions of the likely candidates you might have seen.

THE MAGIC ID FORMULA

1. Note the bird's approximate size.
2. Check its beak.
3. Check its legs.
4. Note bold markings or colours.
5. Note its habitat.
6. Note what it is doing.

JIZZ

This strange word refers to a bird's general shape and size, or the impression it makes when you first see it. It is a good thing to learn the 'jizz' of the various bird families. When we look, for example, at the common Cattle Egret, we know that it belongs to the heron family (as do bitterns), not only because it has long legs and a longish neck (many other bird families have these things) but because of the specific posture of this group of birds: their jizz. Likewise, we all know what a wagtail looks like and how it walks. If you were to see a similar bird with bright blue or pink colouring you would recognise it as a wagtail of sorts because of its strutting walk and bobbing tail: its jizz.

There are often many species of birds within a family. In southern Africa we have 13 robins and 18 related chats and their allies, all of which have a similar jizz.

Robin   Chat   Thrush   Starling

There are 13 different starlings, and they too have a distinctive family jizz, as do sunbirds, bee-eaters, woodpeckers, etc. I cannot stress too strongly the importance of becoming familiar with the jizz of the different bird families as soon as possible. This can be done by studying the birds in your Newman's field vguide. Look carefully at the robins, chats and their allies,

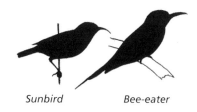

Sunbird   Bee-eater

the rockjumpers and wheatears. They are all quite closely related and share not only similar body shapes and sizes, but also postures such as the tail-up stance and jerky, alert movements.

Study ducks and note how most of them stand with their bodies in the horizontal position. At your local dam, or even at a zoo, you can see how ducks waddle as they walk; this is because their legs are widely spaced and placed in the middle of their bodies. No other

Woodpecker

waterbirds walk in this fashion. These things plus the duck's bill shape all add up to its familiar jizz. In contrast, the whistling ducks, represented by White-faced and Fulvous Ducks, being more closely related to geese, have an erect stance and walk without waddling. This is because their legs are less widely spaced and are placed further back on their bodies.

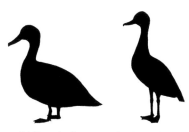

Dabbling duck   Whistling duck

Shrike   Bush shrike   Tchagra   Helmet shrike

Get to know the jizz of the shrikes. Notice their rather bulky bodies, heavy-headed appearance and strong, hooked beaks. Shrikes can also be divided into four distinct groups. True Shrikes, plus the Fiscal Shrike and Sousa's Shrike (*refer to Newman's Birds of Southern Africa*) habitually perch in an exposed position, maybe on a tree or a telephone wire, from where they seize insects on the ground. (This behaviour is known as still–hunting.)

Boubous and bush shrikes tend to seek their food from within the canopies of trees and bushes. Tchagra shrikes mostly forage on the ground or in the lower strata while helmet shrikes flutter in groups from tree to tree. In these cases the birds' identities can be established by a combination of plumage colouring, jizz and habits.

Identify these colourful kingfishers by their beaks. They can be found in Newman's Birds of Southern Africa.

FINDING YOUR WAY AROUND NEWMAN'S FIELDGUIDE

You will avoid endless page turning if you spend some time familiarising yourself with the layout of your Newman's field guide. For instance, if you don't live near the coast you will have little use for the pages showing seabirds, therefore isolate these pages (colour code: dark green) by putting an elastic band around them. This will reduce the number of pages in your field guide until your next holiday at the coast.

The next section covers many inland waterbirds (colour code: yellow), the birds you are likely to see at any dam, lake, river or pond. Spend a little time studying these bird pictures and descriptions before your first wetland visit, then you will have an idea of what to expect.

The next section includes many birds that are water-associated (colour code: red), that is to say they feed on the shorelines or close to water. Some of the species in this section, which includes shorebirds (sometimes called 'waders'), are very difficult for the beginner to identify because they are either rare, secretive or just very similar to each other. Best leave them until you have gained more experience. The birds covered in the rest of this section, including plovers, oystercatchers and stilts are easily seen and identified.

The terrestrial birds are featured in the next section (colour code: light blue), all those you are likely to encounter in grasslands or bush. Some of them will give cause for a little head-scratching unless you get a good look at them; others are quite easy to identify.

A summer flash of brilliant chestnut? Find the flycatchers in Newman's Birds of Southern Africa.

Birds of prey, or raptors (colour code: grey) come next. These birds, from vultures to kestrels, can be both fascinating and very confusing. Get to know them first in the field guide before tackling them in the field. They sometimes confuse even experienced birders, so don't be downhearted!

The next three sections cover various birds from sandgrouse and the pigeon family (colour code: purple) through a variety of colourful birds such as owls (colour code: pink), cuckoos, coucals, louries, rollers, kingfishers, bee-eaters, woodpeckers and barbets (colour code: blue). Also included are some difficult families such as nightjars, swallows and swifts. When tackling these last two groups, do remember that swallows are mostly dark blue above and white underneath, sometimes with some streaking or orange colouring. Swifts are blackish, some with a little white on them. Most important, remember that swallows can perch, but swifts cannot perch and are always seen flying.

All the sections so far discussed have covered non-passerines, with the exception of swallows and one or two others. The rest of the book describes passerines. This section contains the larks and pipits (colour code: orange), which are difficult birds for the beginner, plus all the small- to medium-sized bush birds (colour code: dark pink), the largest among the passerines being the crows. When looking at passerines, remember to examine beak shapes and colours, and plumage details. If the bird has a stout, conical beak it will be a seed-eater (colour code: light green).

An additional section at the end of the species descriptions describes very rare vagrant visitors. Because they are seldom seen they are of interest mostly to very advanced birders.

It is a good idea to memorise the colour code of each section and the groups of birds covered in it. This will facilitate speedy access to the section you want to study.

Describing Birds by

COLOUR

birds with

Black plumage in birds probably serves various functions, according to species. It is certainly true that black birds have distasteful flesh and are therefore not sought after by predators. This may be why black drongos can afford to be so brazen when pestering eagles and other large raptors, even pecking them in flight.

In some species black colouring is a camouflage in their chosen environment. The Black Oystercatcher is difficult to see when feeding on mussel-covered rocks and, when it is incubating its eggs, is almost invisible among dried kelp at the high tide mark, provided it doesn't move.

Black waterbirds, either at the coast or on inland waters, may not be much sought after as tasty meals and are difficult to detect from the air on the dark background of water. Dark plumage also serves many smaller birds since they are difficult to detect in the dark interiors of dense bushes, trees and rocks.

Large black birds have little need for camouflage and can take advantage of their dark plumage in other ways. The Black Eagle, for example, nests during the cold months on the shadow side of mountain cliffs. In such exposed, cold situations the colour black is a good heat retainer.

Swifts, being high-speed airborne feeders, and hole nesters, also have little need for camouflage.

Black Crow

black plumage

THE BIRDS YOU WILL FIND IN THIS CHAPTER

*Long-tailed
Shrike*

black plumage **47**

CAPE CORMORANT
Cape and Namibian coasts. Flocks fly over the sea in long, undulating lines. (Trekduiker) 64 cm

CROWNED CORMORANT
Cape west coast. Like a short-tailed Reed Cormorant with permanent crest. (Kuifkopduiker) 54 cm

BANK CORMORANT
Cape west coast. Small groups on islands and rocks. (Bankduiker) 75 cm

REED CORMORANT
Inland and coastal waters. Brown-speckled wings. (Rietduiker) 60 cm

RUFOUS-BELLIED HERON
Inland waters. Yellow legs, bill and
facial skin. Appears all black.
(Rooipensreier) 58 cm

OPEN-BILLED STORK
Uncommon on inland
waters. Tawny bill with
gap between mandibles.
(Oopbekooievaar) 94 cm

BLACK EGRET
Inland waters. Differs from Slaty Egret in yellow
feet only. Mantles its wings when feeding.
(Swartreier) 66 cm

SPUR-WINGED GOOSE
Inland waters. Pink bill and variable
amount of white.
(Wildemakou) 102 cm

SLATY EGRET
Okavango. Lagoons and backwaters. Told
by yellow legs and feet plus tawny throat.
(Rooikeelreier) 60 cm

black plumage 49

BLACK CRAKE
Inland waters. Small size, yellow bill and red legs. Walks on floating vegetation.
(Swartriethaan) 20-23 cm

RED-KNOBBED COOT
Inland waters. Told by white bill and frontal shield.
(Bleshoender) 43 cm

MOORHEN
Inland waters. White flank marks; red frontal shield and bill; bill-tip and legs yellow.
(Waterhoender) 30-36 cm

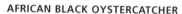

AFRICAN BLACK OYSTERCATCHER
Coastal bird on rocky shores.
Red bill and legs.
(Swarttobie) 51 cm

LESSER MOORHEN
Secluded inland waters. Small shield and culmen red; rest of bill yellow.
(Kleinwaterhoender) 23 cm

BLACK EAGLE
Mountains, cliffs. White 'V' mark on its back; cere and feet yellow.
(Witkruisarend) 84 cm

HELMETED GUINEAFOWL
Bushveld and grassland. Looks black at distance.
(Gewone tarentaal) 53-58 cm

CRESTED GUINEAFOWL
Riverine forests and dense woodland. Pale beak; black tufted head and neck.
(Kuifkoptarentaal) 50 cm

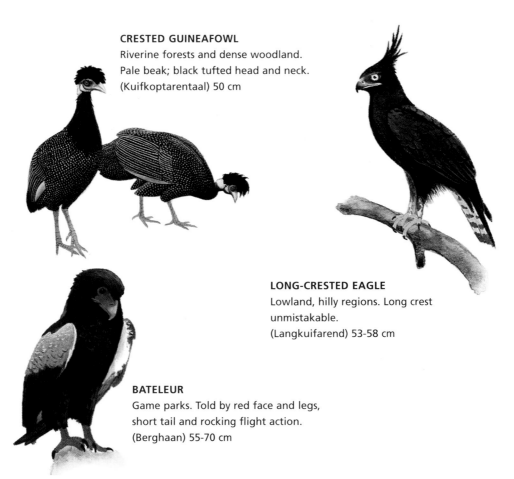

LONG-CRESTED EAGLE
Lowland, hilly regions. Long crest unmistakable.
(Langkuifarend) 53-58 cm

BATELEUR
Game parks. Told by red face and legs, short tail and rocking flight action.
(Berghaan) 55-70 cm

GABAR GOSHAWK
Woodland. Black form uncommon.
All black; cere and legs bright red.
Small, fast flying.
(Witkruissperwer) 30-34 cm

BAT HAWK
Well-wooded rivers. Whitish
eyes, legs and chin. Flies at dusk.
(Vlermuisvalk) 45 cm

BLACK SPARROWHAWK
Black form uncommon. Often found
in gum trees.
(Swartsperwer) 45-58 cm

JACOBIN CUCKOO
Woodland in summer. All black form has
white in wings only. Noisy and active.
(Bontnuwejaarsvoël) 33-34 cm

BLACK HARRIER
Grasslands. Cere, eyes and legs
yellow. Underwing shows white
when hovering.
(Witkruisvleivalk) 48-53 cm

BLACK CUCKOO
Perches and calls in same
tree for long periods.
Diagnostic call 'I'm so SICK'.
(Swartkoekoek) 30 cm

RED-BILLED WOOD HOOPOE
Small flocks in woodland. Curved red bill and long tail. Loud, cackling call. (Gewone kakelaar) 30-36 cm

FORK-TAILED DRONGO
Bushveld. Forked tail diagnostic. (Mikstertbyvanger) 25 cm

SCIMITAR-BILLED WOOD HOOPOE
Woodland. Told by very curved black beak. (Swartbekkakelaar) 24-28 cm

SQUARE-TAILED DRONGO
Forest fringes. Tail has shallow fork only. Wine-red eyes. Noisy. (Kleinbyvanger) 19 cm

GROUND HORNBILL
Large black hornbill with red facial and neck skin. White in wings when flying. (Bromvoël) 90 cm

WHITE-RUMPED SWIFT
Fork-tailed with white crescent shape on lower back. Fast flyer. (Witkruiswindswael) 15 cm

BLACK FLYCATCHER
Woodland. Dark eyes. Tail with small indentation. Quiet bird. (Swartvlieëvanger) 19-22 cm

BLACK CUCKOOSHRIKE
Woodland in summer. Rounded tail and orange-yellow gape. Sometimes with yellow shoulder spot. (Swartkatakoeroe) 22 cm

LITTLE SWIFT
Square tail. Large white patch on rump visible from side. (Kleinwindswael) 14 cm

BLACK SAW-WING SWALLOW
Lowlands and escarpment. Slow, low flight. (Swartsaagvlerkswael) 15 cm

BLACK CROW
Farmlands, open country, often on
telephone poles. Entirely black.
(Swartkraai) 48-53 cm

CARP'S BLACK TIT
Northern Namibia. Like Southern
Black Tit but smaller.
(Ovamboswartmees) 14 cm

WHITE-NECKED RAVEN
Eastern, hilly regions. White patch
on hind neck. Heavy bill.
(Withalskraai) 50-54 cm

SOUTHERN BLACK TIT
Woodland. Female has greyer underparts.
Both sexes have much white in wings.
(Gewone swartmees) 16 cm

HOUSE CROW
Durban. Introduced. Has grey mantle
and breast but looks all black.
(Huiskraai) 43 cm

MOCKING CHAT
Rocky regions. Female has dull red
underparts but seems black.
(Dassievoël) 20-23 cm

BOULDER CHAT
Rocky regions. Zimbabwe and
Botswana. White spots on upper
wing and tail tip.
(Swartberglyster) 23-27 cm

LONG-TAILED SHRIKE
Woodland. Tail shorter in
female. Both sexes have white
wing-stripe.
(Langstertlaksman) 40-50 cm

ANT-EATING CHAT
Well-grazed grasslands. Male darkest.
Flutters up showing pale wing feathers.
(Swartpiek) 18 cm

MOUNTAIN CHAT (female)
Rocky regions. Female dark brown with
white vent and undertail.
Found in scattered groups with males.
(Bergwagter) 17-20 cm

CHESTNUT-FRONTED HELMET SHRIKE
Mostly Mozambique. Appears black. Chestnut forehead; red bill and legs.
(Stekelkophelmlaksman) 19 cm

PALE-WINGED STARLING
Rocky regions in the west. Has orange eyes and white wing-panels with an orange tinge. Often in small flocks.
(Bleekvlerkspreeu) 26 cm

RED-BILLED HELMET SHRIKE
Riverine woodland. Red eye-wattle, bill and legs; white vent and tailtips.
(Swarthelmlaksman) 22 cm

PIED STARLING
Grassveld and Karoo. Pale eyes; orange-yellow gape; white belly and vent.
(Witgatspreeu) 25-27 cm

RED-WINGED STARLING
Widespread. Female has grey head and mantle. Both sexes show brick-red wings in flight.
(Rooivlerkspreeu) 27-28 cm

EUROPEAN STARLING
Southern Cape. Breeding plumage appears black; otherwise greenish, iridescent.
(Europese spreeu) 20-22 cm

RED-COLLARED WIDOW
Bushveld. Breeding male. Red collar often difficult to see unless bird is perched.
(Rooikeelflap) 15-40 cm

SCARLET-CHESTED SUNBIRD
Woodland. Red breast visible when bird is perched. Iridescent green on forehead.
(Rooikeelsuikerbekkie) 15 cm

THICK-BILLED WEAVER
Lowlands. White spots on forehead when breeding.
(Dikbekwewer) 18 cm

RED-SHOULDERED WIDOW
Wetlands. Breeding male.
Red shoulder retained all year.
(Kortstertflap) 19 cm

RED-BILLED BUFFALO WEAVER
Thornveld. Male darker than female.
Both told by red bill.
(Buffelwewer) 24 cm

BLACK SUNBIRD
Woodland and forest. Male all black except for iridescent throat and forehead.
(Swartsuikerbekkie) 15 cm

WHITE-WINGED WIDOW
Bushveld. Breeding male. Yellow
shoulder retained when not breeding.
(Witverkflap) 15-19 cm

YELLOW-RUMPED WIDOW
Marshy regions. Breeding male.
Yellow rump retained when not
breeding.
(Kaapse flap)
15 cm

LONG-TAILED WIDOW
Grasslands. Breeding male.
Tail and red shoulder conspicuous.
(Langstertflap) 60 cm

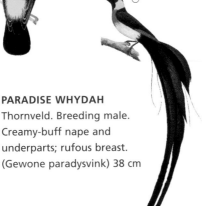

PARADISE WHYDAH
Thornveld. Breeding male.
Creamy-buff nape and
underparts; rufous breast.
(Gewone paradysvink) 38 cm

BLACK WIDOW FINCH (male)
Bushveld. Five almost identical species
when breeding. Told by bill and
leg colours only.
(Blouvinkies) 11 cm

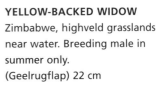

YELLOW-BACKED WIDOW
Zimbabwe, highveld grasslands
near water. Breeding male in
summer only.
(Geelrugflap) 22 cm

black plumage 59

birds with black

When describing black-and-white animals where the black-and-white areas are roughly equal, the term 'pied' is used; thus pied pony, Pied Crow and Pied Babbler. However, this does not apply when either black or white is dominant, as is often the case with birds. For example, the Black Eagle, with so little white on its back, could not be called a pied eagle, and this is the case with many black-and-white birds. Many seabirds have white underparts and blackish upperparts. This colour scheme, also known as counter-shading, acts as a sort of camouflage. From beneath the water the surface appears bright, which means that a white bird is not easily detected by the fish it is trying to catch. From above, the sea appears dark, and a dark bird swimming is difficult to see.

White feathers are less resistant to wear than black feathers, and this is probably the reason why, in most birds, the primary wing feathers (the 'working' feathers during flight) are usually black.

In the context of this book it should be understood that the word 'black' also covers birds that are dark brown, but appear black at a distance.

Pied Kingfisher

MELANISM
Birds may occasionally be encountered with abnormally black or dark brown plumage, a condition known as 'melanism'. This phenomenon can manifest itself as partially or entirely blackish plumage and may occur in a range of species. The loss of normal feather colouring is usually brought about by an excess of a black or brown feather pigment called 'melanin' which darkens the bird's usual feather colouring and may completely mask the individual's normal plumage patterns. In cases of complete melanism, the bird is probably at a disadvantage in courtship since the usual plumage patterns, essential in intra-species recognition, are lacking.

and - white plumage

THE BIRDS YOU WILL FIND IN THIS CHAPTER

KELP GULL
Coastal. Large gull. Yellow bill;
black upperwings; white body.
(Swartrugmeeu) 60 cm

JACKASS PENGUIN
Cape coasts. Black breast-band on
white underparts diagnostic.
(Brilpikkewyn) 63 cm

CASPIAN TERN
Inland waters, coastal lagoons
and estuaries. Black cap; large
red bill; white body.
(Reusesterretjie) 52 cm

CAPE GANNET
Coastal waters. Black legs, tail
and wing feathers on white body;
buffy-yellow on head.
(Witmalgas) 84-94 cm

AFRICAN SKIMMER
Okavango and Zambezi Valley.
Large red bill; short red legs;
body white, upperwings dark.
Skims water, bill immersed.
(Waterploeër) 38 cm

COMMON and ARCTIC TERNS
Coastal. Both similar in non-breeding plumage. Grey above, white below. Arctic Tern has shorter bill and legs.
(Gewone sterretjie) 35 cm
(Arktiese sterretjie) 35 cm

WHITE-BREASTED CORMORANT
All waters. Adult has white throat and breast; immature is entirely white below.
(Witborsduiker) 90 cm

Non-br.

WHISKERED TERN
Inland waters. Non-breeding bird has pale grey upper tail and black line behind eye to black nape.
(Witbaardsterretjie) 23 cm

BLACK-CROWNED NIGHT HERON
Inland waters. Roosts in reeds or trees. Black above; white below; grey wings; yellow legs.
(Gewone nagreier) 56 cm

Non-br.

WHITE-WINGED TERN
Inland waters. Non-breeding bird has white upper tail; black spot behind eye; blackish nape.
(Witvlerksterretjie) 23 cm

SADDLE-BILLED STORK
Inland wetlands. Massive red
and black bill with yellow
saddle diagnostic.
(Saalbekooievaar) 145 cm

WHITE STORK
Grassveld, bushveld. Black and
white with red bill and legs.
Seen in large flocks or small
groups in summer.
(Witooievaar) 117 cm

MARABOU STORK
Bushveld and wetlands.
Massive bill, bare head and neck.
(Maraboe) 152 cm

BLACK STORK
Wetlands. All black excepting
white belly; red bill and legs.
(Grootswartooievaar) 122 cm

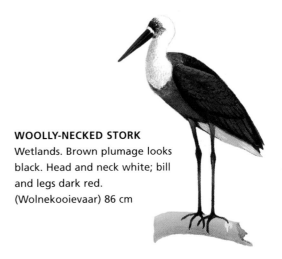

WOOLLY-NECKED STORK
Wetlands. Brown plumage looks
black. Head and neck white; bill
and legs dark red.
(Wolnekooievaar) 86 cm

ABDIM'S STORK
Grassveld and bushveld. White belly,
rump and whitish legs; bill horn-coloured
in summer.
(Kleinswartooievaar) 76 cm

SACRED IBIS
Wetlands. White bird with black
head, neck and down-curved beak.
(Skoorsteenveër) 89 cm

YELLOW-BILLED STORK
Inland waters. Told by yellow
bill plus red face and legs.
(Nimmersat) 97 cm

black-and-white plumage

BLACKSMITH PLOVER
Wetlands, common. Black and white with grey wings; black bill and legs.
(Bontkiewiet) 30 cm

SPUR-WINGED GOOSE
Inland waters. Pink bill and legs. Variable amount of white on face and belly.
(Wildemakou) 102 cm

AVOCET
Wetlands. Entirely pied waterbird. Told by black, upturned bill; legs white.
(Bontelsie) 43 cm

KNOB-BILLED DUCK
Inland waters. Black-speckled head and neck on white underparts; dark blue-green upperparts look black.
(Knobbeleend) 64-79 cm

LONG-TOED PLOVER
Wetlands. Red bill and legs; black-and-white head and breast; white wings in flight.
(Witvlerkkiewiet) 30 cm

BLACK-WINGED STILT
Wetlands. Pied waterbird. Told by long, straight bill and very long red legs.
(Rooipootelsie) 38 cm

LAPPET-FACED VULTURE
Game regions. Dark brown
plumage looks black. Huge size,
red head and neck; yellowish bill;
underparts white.
(Swartaasvoël) 115 cm

BLACK KORHAAN
Grasslands. White ear-patch on black
head; pink bill; tawny upperparts.
(Swartkorhaan) 53 cm

PALM-NUT VULTURE
East coastal regions. White
with black wings and tail;
horn-coloured bill and legs.
(Witaasvoël) 60 cm

OSTRICH (male)
Bushveld and arid lands.
Unmistakable. Tail buff,
grey or white.
(Volstruis) 2 m

WHITE-HEADED VULTURE
Game regions. Dark brown plumage looks
black. Red bill; pink and blue face; pink legs.
(Witkopaasvoël) 85 cm

BLACK-BREASTED SNAKE EAGLE

Bushveld and grasslands. Dark brown plumage looks black. Bare legs. In flight shows pale underwings. (Swartborsslangarend) 63-68 cm

MARTIAL EAGLE

Game regions. Dark brown above, looks black. Legs well feathered. In flight shows dark underwings. (Breëkoparend) 78-83 cm

AUGUR BUZZARD

Wooded hills. Dark brown above; white below; chestnut tail. (Witborsjakkalsvoël) 44-53 cm

AFRICAN HAWK EAGLE

Game regions. Dark brown above, looks black. White below, well spotted. (Grootjagarend) 60-65 cm

BLACK SPARROWHAWK

Tall trees. White form blackish above, white below. Long yellow legs. (Swartsperwer) 46-58 cm

JACOBIN CUCKOO
Woodland. Pied form: black above, white below, with crested head. (Bontnuwejaarsvoël) 33-34 cm

BLACK HARRIER
Moist grasslands. Black with yellow legs. Underwings show much white. (Witkruisvleivalk) 48-53 cm

GREAT SPOTTED CUCKOO
Woodland. Black above, spotted white; white below; grey crested head. (Gevlekte koekoek) 38-40 cm

OSPREY
Inland waters and coastal lagoons. Dark above with facial mask; white below. White legs; long wings. (Visvalk) 55-63 cm

STRIPED CUCKOO
Woodland. Completely pied with streaked breast and crested head. (Gestreepte nuwejaarsvoël) 38-40 cm

THICK-BILLED CUCKOO
Riverine forests. Blackish above, white below; short thick bill; yellow legs. (Dikbekkoekoek) 34cm

PIED KINGFISHER
All waters. Pied with stout black bill.
Hovers over water before plunging.
(Bontvisvanger) 28-29 cm

LITTLE SWIFT
Aerial. Small, blackish, square tail;
white throat; large white rump.
(Kleinwindswael) 14 cm

WHITE-RUMPED SWIFT
Aerial. Blackish, forked tail; white
throat; white crescent shape on back.
(Witkruiswindswael) 15 cm

HORUS SWIFT
Aerial. Black with forked tail;
white throat; large white rump.
(Horuswindswael) 17 cm

GIANT KINGFISHER
Huge pied kingfisher with large
black bill. Rufous breast or belly.
(Reusevisvanger) 43-46 cm

STRIPED KINGFISHER
Woodland. Small blackish and white
bird. Lower mandible and feet red;
blue on back, tail and wings.
(Gestreepte visvanger) 18-19 cm

CROWNED HORNBILL
Riverine forests. Blackish above, white
below; large red bill with yellow base.
(Gekroonde neushoringvoël) 50-57 cm

SOUTHERN YELLOW-BILLED HORNBILL
Savanna. Pied. Large yellow bill unmistakable.
(Geelbekneushoringvoël) 48-60 cm

RED-BILLED HORNBILL
Savanna. Bright red bill and pied
plumage unmistakable.
(Rooibekneushoringvoël) 42-50 cm

TRUMPETER HORNBILL
Riverine forest. Large pied hornbill
with huge bill and casque.
(Gewone boskraai) 58-65 cm

WHITE-EARED BARBET
Lowland tree canopies. Dark
brown but appears black and
white; black bill, legs.
(Witoorhoutkapper) 17 cm

PIED CROW
Widespread. Black crow
with white breast and collar.
(Witborskraai) 46-52 cm

PIED BARBET
Woodland. Above black with yellow
markings; red forehead; black
throat on white underparts.
(Bonthoutkapper) 17-18 cm

BLACK-EARED FINCHLARK (male)
Scrublands. White bill on entirely black
head and body; upperparts rufous.
(Swartoorlewerik) 12-13 cm

AFRICAN PIED WAGTAIL
Wetlands. Small pied bird with bobbing tail.
(Bontkwikkie) 20 cm

CHESTNUT-BACKED FINCHLARK
Short grassland. Black head and body
with white ear-patch and bill in male.
(Rooiruglewerik) 12-13 cm

ASHY TIT
Thornveld. All black and white,
except for grey mantle and body
(Acaciagrysmees) 14 cm

SOUTHERN BLACK TIT
Woodland. Small black bird with
much white in wings.
(Gewone swartmees) 16 cm

NORTHERN GREY TIT
Miombo woodland. Mantle only
grey; rest of bird black and white.
(Miombogrysmees) 14 cm

CARP'S BLACK TIT
Namibian woodland. Small black
bird with much white in wings.
(Ovamboswartmees) 14 cm

RUFOUS-BELLIED TIT
Miombo woodland. A pied tit
with grey mantle and rufous belly.
(Swartkopmees) 15 cm

PIED BABBLER
Woodland. White bird with
black wings and tail; orange eyes.
(Witkatlagter) 26 cm

ARNOT'S CHAT
Mopane woodland. White throat
in female; white cap in male.
Both have white shoulders.
(Bontpiek) 18 cm

MOUNTAIN CHAT (male)
Rocky koppies, dry gullies.
Whitish cap; white vent and
shoulders; rest black.
(Bergwagter) 17-20 cm

MASHONA HYLIOTA
Woodland. Black above with white
wing-patch; pale yellow below.
(Mashonahyliota) 14 cm

CAPPED WHEATEAR
Open veld. Pied terrestrial bird with
rufous upperparts and flanks.
(Hoëveldskaapwagter) 18 cm

FISCAL FLYCATCHER
Woodland. Male black and white,
female brown and white.
(Fiskaalvlieëvanger) 20 cm

MOZAMBIQUE BATIS (male)
Miombo woodland. Small pied bird
with grey cap and yellow eyes.
(Mosambiekbosbontrokkie) 10 cm

PRIRIT BATIS (male)
Thornveld. Small pied bird with
grey cap and yellow eyes.
(Priritbosbontrokkie) 12 cm

CHIN-SPOT BATIS (male)
Woodland. Small pied bird with
grey cap and yellow eyes.
(Witliesbosbontrokkie) 12-13 cm

WATTLE-EYED FLYCATCHER
Thickets. Female has black throat and
chest; male has black breast-band.
(Beloogbosbontrokkie) 18 cm

black-and-white plumage 75

BRUBRU
Woodland. Rufous flanks on white underparts. Female has brown cap and back.
(Bontroklaksman) 15 cm

LONG-TAILED SHRIKE
Woodland. Black, long tail and bold white wing-bar.
(Langstertlaksman) 40-50 cm

FISCAL SHRIKE
Suburbia. Completely pied; stout, hooked beak.
(Fiskaallaksman) 23 cm

PUFFBACK
Woodland. Pied with red eyes. Male puffs out white back.
(Sneeubal) 18 cm

WHITE-TAILED SHRIKE
Woodland. Black and white
with grey mantle and flanks;
yellow eyes.
(Kortstertlaksman) 15 cm

TROPICAL BOUBOU
Woodland. Black above with white
wing-bar; below washed cinnamon.
(Tropiese waterfiskaal) 21 cm

SOUTHERN BOUBOU
Woodland. Black above with white
wing-bar; white throat grades to
cinnamon belly and vent.
(Suidelike waterfiskaal) 23 cm

SWAMP BOUBOU
Riverine woodland. Black above with
white wing-bar; white below.
(Moeraswaterfiskaal) 22-23 cm

DUSKY SUNBIRD (male)
Dry woodland and scrub. Above and breast black with coppery iridescence; belly white. (Namakwasuikerbekkie) 10-12 cm

WHITE HELMET SHRIKE
Bushveld. Pied with grey crown; orange-yellow eye-wattles and legs. (Withelmlaksman) 22 cm

CAPE SPARROW (male)
Suburbia and farmlands. Black and white about head and breast; mantle chestnut. (Gewone mossie) 15 cm

PIED STARLING
Karoo and grasslands. Blackish with white underbelly, vent; whitish eyes; orange gape. (Witgatspreeu) 25-27 cm

BRONZE MANNIKIN
Grass and scrub. Only head and breast black; underparts white; dull brown above.
(Gewone fret) 9cm

PIN-TAILED WHYDAH (breeding male)
Bush and suburbia. Small pied bird with red beak and very long tail.
(Koningrooibekkie) 34 cm

RED-BACKED MANNIKIN
Bush and seeding grasses. Black head and breast; white bill and underparts; rufous upperparts.
(Rooirugfret) 10 cm

BLACK-HEADED CANARY
Dry scrublands. Black of head extends to breast and belly; upperparts rufous.
(Swartkopkanarie) 15 cm

PIED MANNIKIN
Dark brown above; head and thick beak black; white below.
(Dikbekfret) 12-13 cm

birds with

including partially grey

While there are very few completely grey birds in southern Africa, there are numerous species that have partially grey plumage. Most of the birds that fall under this heading qualify by having grey upperparts, such as we see in many gulls, terns and birds of prey. Grey upperparts probably have much the same disruptive value as brown upperparts, as both colours share similar tonal values. In many other birds, grey plumage is seen only on the head, back, wings, tail and so on, and this is less easily understood. The grey heads of bush shrikes, rock thrushes and others are certainly attractive to human observers, but their true value to the bird may be to serve some purpose in mate recognition.

The colour grey, as referred to in this section, is true grey, either pale or dark. Birds that are often referred to as 'grey' are frequently grey-brown or dull brown and will be included only in the section on brown birds.

Grey Lourie

BLUE CRANES
The Blue Crane, an endemic species, was once common and widespread in the moister regions of South Africa. However, in recent years their numbers have so declined that its international status is now defined as 'vulnerable'. Earnest attempts are being made by crane study groups to breed these cranes in captivity for eventual release into the wild, but the process is slow, is based on small numbers of birds and many difficulties have become apparent in the experiment. Known reasons for the Blue Crane's decline are collisions with power lines and deliberate poisoning by crop farmers, but human disturbance at their breeding grounds may also be a contributing factor.

grey plumage

THE BIRDS YOU WILL FIND IN THIS CHAPTER

HARTLAUB'S GULL
Coastal. Grey upperwings and back
only; body white; bill and legs red.
(Hartlaubse meeu) 38 cm

COMMON and ARCTIC TERNS
Coastal. Non-breeding with grey back
and upperwings. Common non-
breeding tern has longer bill and legs.
(Gewone sterretjie) 35cm
(Arktiese sterretjie) 35 cm

GREY-HEADED GULL
Inland and coastal. Grey
head, back and upperwings;
bill and legs red.
(Gryskopmeeu) 42 cm

CASPIAN TERN
Inland waters, coastal lagoons
and estuaries. Grey upperwings
and back; white body; black
cap; large red bill.
(Reusesterretjie) 52 cm

WHISKERED TERN
Inland waters. Completely grey when
breeding; black cap; red bill and legs.
(Witbaardsterretjie) 23 cm

PINK-BACKED PELICAN
Inland waters. Non-breeding bird has grey wings. Paler when breeding. (Kleinpelikaan) 135 cm

SLATY EGRET
Floodpans. Slate-grey with rufous throat; yellow legs and feet. (Rooikeelreier) 60 cm

DWARF BITTERN
Wetlands. Upperparts dark grey; underparts streaked grey. (Dwergrietreier) 25 cm

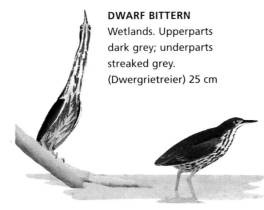

BLACK-CROWNED NIGHT HERON
Wetlands. Grey upperwings and tail; crown and back black; body white; legs yellow. (Gewone nagreier) 56 cm

GREEN-BACKED HERON
Inland waters. Mantle and underbody grey; black cap; dark wings and tail; legs orange. (Groenrugreier) 41 cm

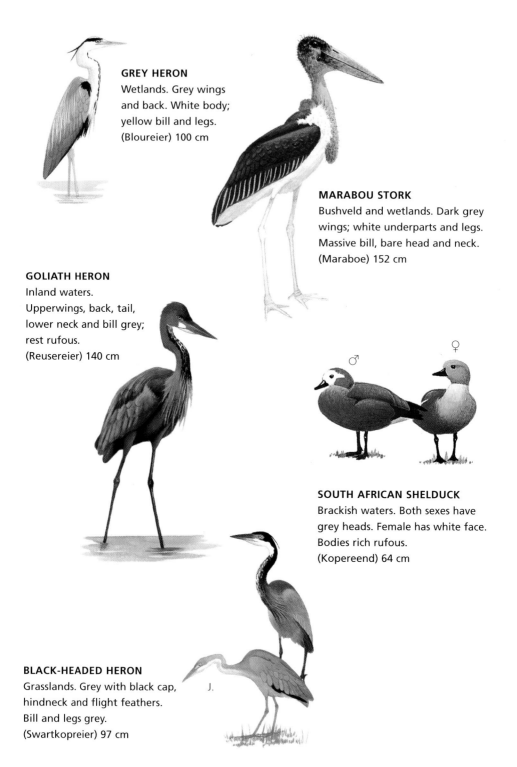

GREY HERON
Wetlands. Grey wings
and back. White body;
yellow bill and legs.
(Bloureier) 100 cm

MARABOU STORK
Bushveld and wetlands. Dark grey
wings; white underparts and legs.
Massive bill, bare head and neck.
(Maraboe) 152 cm

GOLIATH HERON
Inland waters.
Upperwings, back, tail,
lower neck and bill grey;
rest rufous.
(Reusereier) 140 cm

SOUTH AFRICAN SHELDUCK
Brackish waters. Both sexes have
grey heads. Female has white face.
Bodies rich rufous.
(Kopereend) 64 cm

BLACK-HEADED HERON
Grasslands. Grey with black cap,
hindneck and flight feathers.
Bill and legs grey.
(Swartkopreier) 97 cm

AFRICAN RAIL
Reedbeds. Lateral head
and underparts grey;
upperparts rufous; bill,
legs red.
(Grootriethaan) 36 cm

BLACKSMITH PLOVER
Wetlands. Grey wings on otherwise
black-and-white bird.
(Bontkiewiet) 30 cm

BLACK-WINGED PLOVER
Grassveld. Grey head (white forehead),
neck and upper breast; above brown,
below white.
(Grootswartvlerkkiewiet) 29 cm

WHITE-CROWNED PLOVER
Rivers. Lateral head and neck grey;
crown and underparts white;
wings black and white; bill,
wattles, legs yellow.
(Witkopkiewiet) 30 cm

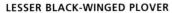

LESSER BLACK-WINGED PLOVER
Grassveld and woodland. Grey head;
(small) white forehead, neck and upper
breast; above brown, below white.
(Kleinswartvlerkkiewiet) 23 cm

BLUE KORHAAN
Grassveld. Neck and body blue-grey; upperparts tawny-brown.
(Bloukorhaan) 50-58 cm

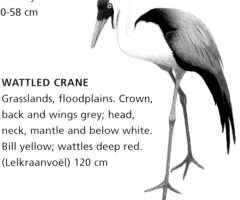

WATTLED CRANE
Grasslands, floodplains. Crown, back and wings grey; head, neck, mantle and below white. Bill yellow; wattles deep red.
(Lelkraanvoël) 120 cm

BLUE CRANE
Grasslands, vleis. All blue-grey except white crown, black wing-feathers. Bill yellowish.
(Bloukraanvoël) 105 cm

HELMETED GUINEAFOWL
Grasslands and bush. Blue neck; red helmet; casque and bill horn-coloured.
(Gewone tarentaal) 53-58 cm

CROWNED CRANE
Grasslands, marshes. Neck and body grey; yellow crest on black crown; white facial patch.
(Mahem) 105 cm

SECRETARYBIRD
Grasslands. Red or orange face; flight feathers, upper legs and tailtip black; legs pink. (Sekretarisvoël) 125-150 cm

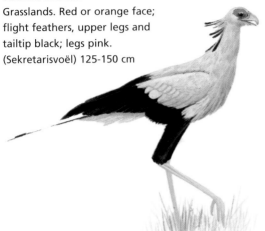

LIZARD HAWK
Woodland. Upperparts, upper chest grey; underparts banded. Black throat-stripe; red cere and legs; bold white band on black tail. (Akkedisvalk) 35-37 cm

WESTERN BANDED SNAKE EAGLE
Riverine forests. Head to lower breast ash-grey; soft parts yellow. (Enkelbandslangarend) 55 cm

BLACK-SHOULDERED KITE
Woodland, general. Above grey with black carpal patches; below white; black wingtips. (Blouvalk) 30 cm

SOUTHERN BANDED SNAKE EAGLE
Riverine forests. Head to upper breast ash-grey; soft parts yellow. (Dubbelbandslangarend) 60 cm

LITTLE SPARROWHAWK
Woodland. Above grey; tail black with two white spots; below banded rufous; soft parts yellow. (Kleinsperwer) 23-25 cm

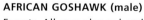

AFRICAN GOSHAWK (male)
Forests. All grey above; banded rufous below; cere grey; eyes and legs yellow. (Afrikaanse sperwer) 36 cm

LITTLE BANDED GOSHAWK
Woodland. Plain grey above; banded rufous below; eyes deep red; cere and legs yellow.
(Gebande sperwer) 30-34 cm

PALE CHANTING GOSHAWK
Karoo, semi-desert. Pale grey above; secondaries and rump white; primaries and tail black; chest grey; belly finely barred. Cere and legs coral-red. (Bleeksingvalk) 53-63 cm

GABAR GOSHAWK
Woodland. Above and breast grey; bold white rump; eyes deep red, cere and legs red.
(Witkruissperwer) 30-34 cm

DARK CHANTING GOSHAWK
Woodland. Dark grey above; rump white barred grey; primaries and tail black; dark grey breast and finely barred under-parts; coral-pink cere and legs. (Donkersingvalk) 50-56 cm

OVAMBO SPARROWHAWK
Woodland. Above grey, below banded grey to throat; eyes dark; cere red, legs orange.
(Ovambosperwer) 33-40 cm

PYGMY FALCON
Thorn savanna. Grey above (female with rufous mantle); white below; red soft parts.
(Dwergvalk) 19,5 cm

PALLID HARRIER
Grasslands. Above pale grey; below white; primaries narrow, black. Soft parts yellow.
(Witborsvleivalk) 44-48 cm

LANNER FALCON
Grey above; russet crown; buffy-white below; orbital rings, cere and legs yellow.
(Edelvalk) 40-45 cm

MONTAGU'S HARRIER
Grasslands. Above grey; wings with central black bars; broad black primaries. Chest grey; belly and underwings white, streaked rufous.
(Blouvleivalk) 40-47 cm

DICKINSON'S KESTREL
Palm savanna. Grey all over; head paler; wings darker; soft parts yellow.
(Dickinsonse valk) 28-30 cm

GYMNOGENE
Woodland. Wings grey, edged black above and below; tail all black with white band; breast grey; underparts banded. Cere and legs yellow.
(Kaalwangvalk) 60-66 cm

ROCK KESTREL (male)
Hills. Rufous body; grey head and tail; tail with black tip; soft parts yellow.
(Kransrooivalk) 30-33 cm

LESSER KESTREL (male)
Grassland, Karoo. Grey head, back and tail; grey on upper wings; rest rufous. Soft parts yellow.
(Kleinrooivalk) 28-30 cm

WESTERN RED-FOOTED KESTREL (male)
Grasslands. Dark grey above and below; rufous vent. Soft parts red.
(Westelike rooipootvalk) 28-30 cm

EASTERN RED-FOOTED KESTREL
Grasslands. Both sexes grey above; male pale grey below (rufous vent); female white, well spotted. Soft parts red or orange.
(Oostelike rooipootvalk) 28-30 cm

CAPE TURTLE DOVE
General. Greyest of the collared doves; narrow collar and bill black; legs dark red.
(Gewone tortelduif) 28 cm

GREY LOURIE
Woodland. All grey with
crested head; soft parts black.
(Kwêvoël) 47-50 cm

WHITE-FACED OWL
Woodland. All grey; white
facial disc with black surround;
eyes orange.
(Witwanguil) 25-28 cm

RED-CHESTED CUCKOO
Woodland, suburbia. Grey
upperparts; brick-red breast;
banded below. Orbital ring,
lower mandible and legs yellow.
(Piet-my-vrou) 28 cm

GIANT EAGLE OWL
Woodland. All grey, paler
below. Facial disc with
black outline; eyes dark;
eyelids pink.
(Reuse-ooruil) 60-65 cm

AFRICAN SCOPS OWL
Woodland. Grey plumage
streaked black resembles tree
bark; prominent 'ear' tufts.
Eyes yellow.
(Skopsuil) 18 cm

WHITE-BACKED MOUSEBIRD
Thornveld. Grey above with white rump; buff below; bill white tipped black; feet red.
(Witkruismuisvoël) 30-34 cm

CAPE WAGTAIL
Wetlands and suburbia. All greyish; chin and throat white with black chest-band.
(Gewone kwikkie) 18 cm

GREY-HOODED KINGFISHER
Woodland, mixed bushveld. Head, mantle and upper breast grey; belly chestnut-brown; wings black and blue; tail blue; bill and legs red.
(Gryskopvisvanger) 20 cm

WHITE-BREASTED CUCKOOSHRIKE
Mature woodland. Blue-grey above; white below; male with grey throat. Upper tail and soft parts black.
(Witborskatakoeroe) 27 cm

LONG-TAILED WAGTAIL
Mountain streams. Very long tail. Above grey and black; below white; black chest-band.
(Bergkwikkie) 19-20 cm

GREY CUCKOOSHRIKE
Forest fringes. Dark grey all over; flight feathers, tail and soft parts black.
(Bloukatakoeroe) 27 cm

HOUSE CROW
Durban region. Rear head, breast and mantle grey; rest black.
(Huiskraai) 43 cm

MIOMBO ROCK THRUSH (male)
Miombo woodland. Grey head and upperparts flecked black; breast dull orange grading to white belly.
(Angolakliplyster) 18 cm

ASHY TIT
Zimbabwe thornveld. Mantle and underparts grey; cap, throat, central belly and tail black.
(Acaciagrysmees) 14 cm

SENTINEL ROCK THRUSH (male)
Rocky hills or grasslands. Chest, head and mantle grey; underparts dull orange.
(Langtoonkliplyster) 21 cm

SHORT-TOED ROCK THRUSH (male)
Rocky hills. Back, mantle and throat grey; cap white; underparts dull orange.
(Korttoonkliplyster) 18 cm

CAPE ROCK THRUSH (male)
Cliffs. Head only grey; rest of body, including mantle, dull orange.
(Kaapse kliplyster) 21 cm

MOUNTAIN CHAT (male)
Rocky hills. All grey except white shoulder and vent; wings black.
(Bergwagter) 17-20 cm

LAYARD'S TITBABBLER
Fynbos and mountain scrub. Dark grey above; white below with spotted breast; pale eyes.
(Grystjeriktik) 15 cm

KAROO CHAT
Karoo scrub. Generally grey but for white belly; wings, upper tail blackish. Western race paler, buffy.
(Karoospekvreter) 15-18 cm

NEDDICKY (S and SE race)
Woodland and thickets. Cap rust-brown; rest of upperparts brown; underparts blue-grey.
(Neddikkie) 10-11 cm

TITBABBLER
Thorn thickets. Mostly dark grey with pale eye and chestnut vent; breast spotted.
(Bosveldtjeriktik) 15 cm

FAN-TAILED FLYCATCHER
Woodland. Mantle and back grey;
tail black with white outer feathers;
wings blackish; white underbelly.
(Waaierstertvlieëvanger) 14 cm

FAIRY FLYCATCHER
Karoo. Grey cap and upper body; black
tail; mask and black wings with white
bar; pink central breast.
(Feevlieëvanger) 12 cm

BLUE-GREY FLYCATCHER
Riverine woodland. Grey above;
pale grey below; wings blackish.
(Blougrysvlieëvanger) 14-15 cm

PARADISE FLYCATCHER
Woodland and suburbia. Deep
blue-grey crested head grades to
grey breast; upperparts and tail
chestnut-brown; orbital ring and
bill blue.
(Paradysvlieëvanger) 23-41 cm

BOKMAKIERIE
Suburbia. Grey crown and mantle;
rest green above, yellow below;
bold black breast-band.
(Bokmakierie) 23 cm

RED-BACKED SHRIKE (male)
Bushveld. Grey cap and nape;
chestnut back; black mask, wings and
tail; white below; hooked beak.
(Rooiruglaksman) 18 cm

LESSER GREY SHRIKE
Bushveld. Above grey and black;
below white; stout hooked beak.
(Gryslaksman) 20-22 cm

GREY-HEADED BUSH SHRIKE
Woodland. Grey hood; heavy, hooked
bill; upperparts green; below yellow;
breast orange; eyes yellow.
(Spookvoël) 25-27 cm

GREY SUNBIRD
Coastal forests. Entirely grey, darker
above; slender, down-curved beak.
(Gryssuikerbekkie) 14 cm

SOUTHERN GREY-HEADED SPARROW
Woodland. Grey head; upperparts chestnut;
below whitish. Stout conical bill black
or horn-coloured
(Gryskopmossie) 15-16 cm

GREY WAXBILL
Woodland thickets. Grey, darker above
with red eyes, rump and upper tail-base.
(Gryssysie) 11 cm

CAPE SPARROW (female)
Suburbia, farmlands. Grey and white head
extends to upper breast; mantle chestnut;
wings black and white; underparts whitish;
stout bill black.
(Gewone mossie) 15 cm

STREAKY-HEADED CANARY
Woodland. Grey-brown above; streaky
crown; white eyebrow; stout blackish
bill; white below.
(Streepkopkanarie) 16 cm

birds with

including partially white

M ost white birds are waterbirds. Certainly there are many white or partially white seabirds that do not fall within the scope of this book, but there are others that occur on inland waters and at the coast. Perhaps the most familiar of these white birds is the common Cattle Egret that is seen with grazing cattle in farmlands and even in our towns. There are other white egrets, their plumages all so similar that they can cause much confusion until their specific differences are learnt. (Remember that egrets are merely a type of heron.) White plumage is strikingly bright and renders the bird highly conspicuous under normal African conditions. In northern regions, however, where the lands are often snow-bound for months, some birds actually benefit from the camouflage afford-ed by white plumage. This is certainly not the case with white African birds, so there must be another reason for their being white. One theory is that waterbirds are reasonably safe while standing in water since few land predators habitually hunt in water. A second theory suggests that, for a bird that forages fully exposed to the hot sun for much of the day, white feathers are the best heat reflectors.

Eastern White Pelican

white plumage

THE BIRDS YOU WILL FIND IN THIS CHAPTER

Greater Flamingo

BIRD TERRITORIES

A territory is a region a bird or pair of birds defends against conspecifics (others of its kind) for purposes of feeding and breeding. The territory may be very small in communal breeders, perhaps half a hectare in songbirds, or may cover many square kilometres in some eagles. The male bird must select a territory of a size that is defensible and yet provide sufficient food for itself, its mate and their young.

Many small birds only defend the area of the nest site (as in many weavers) and forage for food further afield. Communal feeders, such as gulls, terns and many other ground-nesting waterbirds, space their nests closely but just out of pecking range of their immediate neighbours. Even in a crowded colony each bird is able to identify and fly directly to its own nest without interacting with those around. In contrast, the Cape Gannet, which nests in densely-packed island colonies, requires a fairly long take-off run into wind to get airborne. In order to move through the colony to the take-off point, without being molested by the others, a departing bird must adopt a non-aggressive posture called 'sky-pointing'. The head and neck are held vertically while the bird walks between all the other nests. Should its head be lowered, even briefly, those around it will interpret the action as an aggressive one and it will be treated to a roughing-up until it readopts the sky-pointing posture.

HARTLAUB'S GULL
Coastal. Mostly white; grey
upperwings; black wingtips;
red bill and legs.
(Hartlaubse meeu) 38cm

LITTLE EGRET
Wetlands. All white;
black bill and legs;
feet yellow.
(Kleinwitreier) 64 cm

EASTERN WHITE PELICAN
Estuaries, lagoons. Adult all white; yellowish
bill; pink legs. Black flight feathers.
(Witpelikaan) 180 cm

INTERMEDIATE EGRET
Wetlands. All white; bill yellow; upper legs
dull yellow; lower legs black.
(Geelbekwitreier) 68 cm

CATTLE EGRET
Pastures. All white except in summer
when buff on head, neck and back.
Bill, legs yellow to pink.
(Veereier) 54 cm

GREAT WHITE HERON
Wetlands. Bill yellow, black briefly
when breeding; legs and feet black.
(Grootwitreier) 95 cm

BLACK-SHOULDERED KITE
Grasslands. Below white; wingtips black.
Above grey; black shoulder-patches.
(Blouvalk) 30 cm

GREATER FLAMINGO
Salt pans and soda lakes. White with
pink and black bill; long pink legs;
red and black wings.
(Grootflamink) 140 cm

PALLID HARRIER
Grasslands. Above pale grey; below
white. At distance appears all white.
(Witborsvleivalk) 44 -48 cm

AFRICAN SPOONBILL
Wetlands. White with red face;
red and grey spatulate bill; red legs.
(Lepelaar) 91 cm

MARTIAL EAGLE (immature)
Woodland, bushveld. Underparts
white; upperparts brown.
Feet yellow.
(Breëkoparend) 78-83 cm

WATTLED STARLING
Open bushveld. Male whitish
when breeding; head ornamented
with black and yellow; tail black.
(Lelspreeu) 21 cm

birds with

*including partially blue
plumage or blue bills*

S ome of our most colourful birds owe their
brilliance to blue plumage – often iridescent
blue as seen, for example, in the glossy
starlings, which appear metallic blue or green according to the light.

There are many birds, large and small, with dark blue plumage that appears black in all but the most favourable sunlight, which emphasises the iridescent gloss in the feathers. Among these are swallows and wood hoopoes. Many of the larger 'black' birds, such as the Spur-winged Goose, crows and certain raptors, may also appear blue-black in full sun.

Iridescence is produced by a thin layer of a substance called keratin, which occurs on the surface of the feather-barbules, or by minute granules of melanin that occur in a thin layer just below the surface of the feather-barbules. Iridescent feathers are not normally found in a bird's flight feathers.

Rollers exhibit brilliant blue wings, often described as electric blue. This is a true colour which also occurs in some bee-eaters. This non-iridescent colour is created by the scattering of light when it passes through minute air-filled cavities in the keratin of the barbules. As a result, no matter at what angle, the colour does not change.

NEST SANITATION

In the early chick-rearing period of most passerine birds, the disposal of excreta is important in the interests of nest cleanliness and the safety of the brood since predators are likely to be attracted by both smell and the sight of accumulated white droppings. In a group of small birds, the chicks of which are confined to the nest for some weeks, the chicks' faeces are excreted in a thin but strong mucous sac, which is either swallowed by the parents or disposed of far away from the nest.

The more mobile nestlings of raptors, herons, kingfishers and others, eject their faeces from the nest in liquid form with some force.

blue plumage

THE BIRDS YOU WILL FIND IN THIS CHAPTER

*Blue
Swallow*

BALD IBIS
Montane grassland. Iridescent
blue-black plumage; red cap,
bill and legs.
(Kalkoenibis) 79 cm

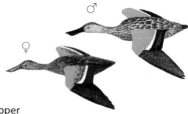

CAPE SHOVELLER
Wetlands. Pale blue upper
forewings seen in flight;
brightest in male.
(Kaapse slopeend) 53 cm

HOTTENTOT TEAL
Wetlands. Small, brown-capped
duck with blue-grey bill.
(Gevlekte eend) 35 cm

MACCOA DUCK (male)
Wetlands. Bright blue bill on
black head; body chestnut.
(Bloubekeend) 46 cm

KNOB-BILLED DUCK
Wetlands. Iridescent blue above;
white below; head speckled black.
(Knobbeleend) 64-79 cm

BLUE CRANE
Grasslands. All grey-blue except white crown and black wing feathers. Bill yellowish.
(Bloukraanvoël) 105 cm

PURPLE GALLINULE
Wetlands. Above green; head and below blue; frontal shield and bill red; legs pink.
(Grootkoningriethaan) 46 cm

HELMETED GUINEAFOWL
Grasslands and bush. Blue neck; red helmet; casque and bill horn-coloured.
(Gewone tarentaal) 53-58 cm

LESSER GALLINULE
Wetlands. Above green; head and below blue; frontal shield blue; bill and legs red.
(Kleinkoningriethaan) 25 cm

CRESTED GUINEAFOWL
Riverine thickets. Black body with blue spots and stripes.
(Kuifkoptarentaal) 50 cm

BLUE KORHAAN
Grassveld. Neck and body grey-blue, upperwings tawny-brown.
(Bloukorhaan) 50-58 cm

KNYSNA LOURIE

Forest. Folded wings and upper tail iridescent blue; rest of body green; wings red in flight. (Knysnaloerie) 47 cm

MEYER'S PARROT

Woodland. Back and rump pale blue; head, mantle and wings brown; below green. (Bosveldpapegaai) 23 cm

PURPLE-CRESTED LOURIE

Woodland. Crest blue-purple; wings and upper tail iridescent blue; body matt green with orange wash; wings red in flight. (Bloukuifloerie) 47 cm

RÜPPELL'S PARROT

Woodland. Back, underbelly and vent deep blue, rest of body and wings dark brown. (Bloupenspapegaai) 23 cm

RED-BREASTED SWALLOW
Grass savanna. Above metallic blue; below deep orange.
(Rooiborsswael) 24 cm

GREATER STRIPED SWALLOW
Grassland. Top of head orange; rump pale orange; rest of upperparts metallic blue; below whitish, lightly streaked.
(Grootstreepswael) 20 cm

MOSQUE SWALLOW
Woodland. Above metallic blue; throat, upper breast and underwings white; rest of underbody deep orange.
(Moskeeswael) 23 cm

LESSER STRIPED SWALLOW
Bushveld. Upper half of head and rump orange; rest of upperparts metallic blue; below white, heavily streaked.
(Kleinstreepswael) 16 cm

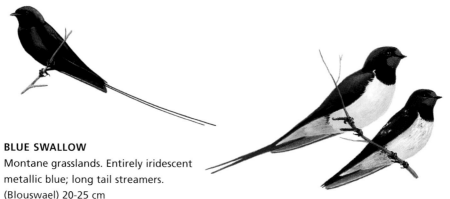

BLUE SWALLOW
Montane grasslands. Entirely iridescent
metallic blue; long tail streamers.
(Blouswael) 20-25 cm

EUROPEAN SWALLOW
Aerial. Above metallic blue; forehead and
chin orange; throat black; below white.
Forked tail.
(Europese swael) 18 cm

SOUTH AFRICAN CLIFF SWALLOW
Bridges, towers. Cap brownish; rump orange;
rest of upperparts dull metallic blue; breast
orange dappled dark blue; belly white;
vent orange.
(Familieswael) 15 cm

WHITE-THROATED SWALLOW
Wetlands. Orange forehead;
metallic-blue above; white below
with black breast-band; forked tail.
(Witkeelswael) 17 cm

WIRE-TAILED SWALLOW
Rivers. Above metallic blue; cap orange;
below white; long tail streamers.
(Draadstertswael) 13 cm

PEARL-BREASTED SWALLOW
Open woodland; above metallic blue;
below white; forked tail.
(Pêrelborsswael) 14 cm

SWALLOW-TAILED BEE-EATER
Woodland. Blue collar, upper tail and
belly; throat yellow; rest green.
Forked tail.
(Swaelstertbyvreter) 20-22 cm

GREY-RUMPED SWALLOW
River banks and grassy slopes.
Above metallic blue, except greyish
cap and rump. Forked tail.
(Gryskruisswael)
14 cm

CARMINE BEE-EATER
Rivers and bushveld. Blue cap and
underbelly; rest of body carmine-red.
(Rooiborsbyvreter) 33-38 cm

HOUSE MARTIN
Aerial. Above metallic blue with
white rump; below white.
Tail with shallow fork.
(Huisswael) 14 cm

blue plumage **109**

EUROPEAN BEE-EATER
Aerial. Forehead and underbody
blue; throat yellow; upperparts
chestnut and green.
(Europese byvreter) 25-29 cm

GREY-HOODED KINGFISHER
Woodland. Back, tail and wings royal blue;
wing coverts black; head and mantle grey;
belly chestnut; bill red.
(Gryskopvisvanger) 20 cm

BLUE-CHEEKED BEE-EATER
Wetlands. Eyebrows, cheeks, rump
and belly blue; above green;
chin yellow; throat chestnut.
(Blouwangbyvreter) 27-33 cm

BROWN-HOODED KINGFISHER
Woodland. Upper body and tail blue;
upper wings blue and black; head
and mantle streaked brownish;
below white; bill red.
(Bruinkopvisvanger) 23-24 cm

WOODLAND KINGFISHER
Woodland. Above turquoise-blue;
wing coverts black; below white;
bill red and black.
(Bosveldvisvanger) 23-24 cm

STRIPED KINGFISHER
Woodland. Back and tail blue; wings blue
above; coverts black; cap streaked brown;
below white; flanks streaked;
bill dark brown and red.
(Gestreepte visvanger) 18-19 cm

MALACHITE KINGFISHER
Wetlands. Above blue; below orange-buff;
white ear-patch and throat; bill and legs red.
(Kuifkopvisvanger) 14 cm

PYGMY KINGFISHER
Woodland. Above entirely deep
blue; below buff; cheeks mauve;
bill and feet red.
(Dwergvisvanger) 13 cm

HALF-COLLARED KINGFISHER
Rivers. Brilliant blue above; below
throat white; underparts buffy;
bill black; legs red.
(Blouvisvanger) 20 cm

EUROPEAN ROLLER
Woodland. Blue head and
underparts; square tail.
(Europese troupant) 30-31 cm

RACKET-TAILED ROLLER
Woodland. Plain blue below;
spatulate tail-shafts.
(Knopsterttroupant) 36 cm

BROAD-BILLED ROLLER
Woodland. Blue vent and tail;
deep blue wings; yellow bill.
(Geelbektroupant) 27 cm

LILAC-BREASTED ROLLER
Woodland. Blue belly and tail;
blue wings; lilac breast.
(Gewone troupant) 36 cm

PURPLE ROLLER
Woodland. Deep blue tail
and wings; below streaked
white on maroon.
(Groottroupant) 36-40 cm

RED-BILLED WOOD HOOPOE
Woodland. Deep iridescent blue;
head green and blue; curved red bill;
long tail.
(Gewone kakelaar)
30-36 cm

BLACK CROW
Farmlands. Entirely
metallic blue-black.
(Swartkraai) 48-53 cm

PARADISE FLYCATCHER
Woodland. Head blue-black;
orbital ring and bill bright blue.
(Paradysvlieëvanger) 23-41 cm

SCIMITAR-BILLED WOOD HOOPOE
Woodland. Deep iridescent purple-blue;
well-curved black bill.
(Swartbekkakelaar) 24-28 cm

TRUMPETER HORNBILL
Riverine forests. Breast and
upperparts deep metallic blue;
huge bill with casque.
(Gewone boskraai) 58-65 cm

LONG-TAILED GLOSSY STARLING
Mopane woodland. Iridescent purple-blue;
long, graduated tail; dark eyes.
(Langstertglansspreeu) 30-34 cm

GREATER BLUE-EARED GLOSSY STARLING
Woodland. Head and breast glossy blue;
wings glossy green; flanks and belly purple;
eyes yellow.
(Groot-blouoorglansspreeu) 21-23 cm

LESSER BLUE-EARED GLOSSY STARLING
Miombo woodland. Glossy blue-green;
flanks purple; eyes yellow.
(Klein-blouoorglansspreeu) 20 cm

BURCHELL'S GLOSSY STARLING
Savanna. Iridescent blue and purple,
black mask and dark eyes.
(Grootglansspreeu) 30-34 cm

SHARP-TAILED GLOSSY STARLING
Woodland. Glossy blue; wings greener; graduated tail; reddish eyes.
(Spitsstertglansspreeu) 26 cm

BLUE WAXBILL
Thornveld. Underparts blue; above brown.
(Gewone blousysie) 12-14 cm

CAPE GLOSSY STARLING
Woodland and suburbia. Glossy blue-green; head bluer; yellow eyes.
(Kleinglansspreeu) 23-25 cm

VIOLET-EARED WAXBILL
Thornveld. Forehead and upper tail coverts blue; side of head violet; red bill.
(Koningblousysie) 13-15 cm

WHITE-BELLIED SUNBIRD (male)
Wooded regions. Head, breast and mantle glossy blue; belly white; curved black bill.
(Witpenssuikerbekkie) 11 cm

blue plumage **115**

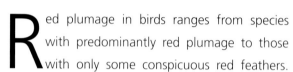

birds with

Red plumage in birds ranges from species with predominantly red plumage to those with only some conspicuous red feathers. A predominance of red makes a bird conspicuous. Usually this occurs in the male of the species and often, but not always, during the breeding season only. The male Red Bishop in breeding plumage, actively displaying with feathers fluffed out, serves both to deflect attention from the incubating female and as a warning to other Red Bishop males to stay away. Where the plumage is only partially red it is often found on the head or breast, or both, as seen in the Black-collared Barbet. Since this is the part of the bird presented to a rival, or to a mate, it may serve either as a warning signal or as mate recognition. Where a bird has a red cap, head or rump, its function is less obvious, but the colour may be used during courtship displays and in a variety of subtle interaction behaviours between individuals about which we understand little. The red cap or forehead of many woodpeckers, which is prominently displayed when the bird is peering from its nest-hole, probably serves to warn other woodpeckers that the territory is occupied. The brilliant red wings of the forest-dwelling Knysna Lourie serves well as a recognition feature for others in the group in dense foliage. The red colouring in the wings of many louries comes from a chemical called turacin. The name 'turaco', which is used for these birds outside southern Africa, comes from this chemical. Turacin is responsible for the red colouring in other birds too. Birds that have red bills, red legs or facial skin are discussed in the following chapter.

red plumage

THE BIRDS YOU WILL FIND IN THIS CHAPTER

Red-headed Weaver

ROSY-FACED LOVEBIRD
Rocky gorges. Red forecrown,
face and neck on green bird;
white bill.
(Rooiwangparkiet) 17-18 cm

LILIAN'S LOVEBIRD
Woodland. Red forecrown, face,
neck and bill on green bird.
(Niassaparkiet) 17-18 cm

LESSER FLAMINGO
Salt pans. Pink bird with red
wing feathers, bill and legs.
(Kleinflamink) 102 cm

ROCK PIGEON
Cliffs. Deep reddish wings spotted
white; red facial skin and legs.
(Kransduif) 33 cm

GREATER FLAMINGO
Wetlands. Red wings on white
bird; bill and legs pink.
(Grootflamink) 140 cm

NARINA TROGON

Forests. Scarlet-red underparts on iridescent green bird; bill yellowish. (Bosloerie) 29-34 cm

CARMINE BEE-EATER

Riverine bush. Carmine-red body and wings; curved black bill. (Rooiborsbyvreter) 33-38 cm

KNYSNA LOURIE

Forests. Scarlet-red wings on green bird; red bill. (Knysnaloerie) 47 cm

WHITE-FRONTED BEE-EATER

Rivers. Red throat on tawny underparts; curved black bill. (Rooikeelbyvreter) 22-24 cm

PURPLE-CRESTED LOURIE

Woodland. Crimson-red wings on blue-green bird; black bill. (Bloukuifloerie) 47 cm

PIED BARBET
Woodland. Forecrown only red;
rest black, white and yellow.
(Bonthoutkapper)
17-18 cm

RED-FRONTED TINKER BARBET
Woodland. Red forehead (front) on
black and yellow upperparts.
(Rooiblestinker) 10,5 cm

BLACK-COLLARED BARBET
Woodland. Red crown, cheeks,
throat and breast; black collar.
(Rooikophoutkapper) 19-20 cm

GROUND WOODPECKER
Rocks. Rump red; below streaked
red on buff. Pale eyes, grey head.
(Grondspeg) 26 cm

♂

OLIVE WOODPECKER
Forests. Red cap (male);
red rump both sexes;
grey head.
(Gryskopspeg) 18-20 cm

♀

CRESTED BARBET
Woodland. Red speckles on yellow head
and breast; red rump; black-crested head.
(Kuifkophoutkapper) 23 cm

GOLDEN-TAILED WOODPECKER
Woodland. Male with red cap and moustachial streak; female with red nape only; streaked black below.
(Goudstertspeg) 20-23 cm

CARDINAL WOODPECKER (male)
Woodland. Red cap; brown forehead; streaked black below.
(Kardinaalspeg) 14-16 cm

BEARDED WOODPECKER (male)
Woodland. Red crown; black forehead; banded below.
(Baardspeg) 23-25 cm

BENNETT'S WOODPECKER
Woodland. Male with red cap and moustachial streak; female with red nape; brown face and throat; below lightly spotted.
(Bennettse speg) 22-24 cm

KNYSNA WOODPECKER
Coastal bush. Male with red cap and moustachial streak; female with black cap and red nape; both well spotted below.
(Knysnaspeg) 20 cm

LESSER DOUBLE-COLLARED SUNBIRD (male)
General. Narrow red lower breast-band; belly dull grey-buff; head and mantle glossy-green.
(Kleinrooibandsuikerbekkie) 12,5 cm

PINK-THROATED LONGCLAW
Moist grassland. Red chin and throat; red central breast and belly; black breast-band.
(Rooskeelkalkoentjie) 20 cm

GREATER DOUBLE-COLLARED SUNBIRD (male)
Montane. Wide red lower breast-band; belly dull grey-buff; head and mantle glossy-green.
(Grootrooibandsuikerbekkie) 14 cm

CRIMSON-BREASTED BOUBOU
Thornveld. Crimson below; black above with white wing-stripe.
(Rooiborslaksman) 22-23 cm

GORGEOUS BUSH SHRIKE
Mixed bush. Red chin and throat; bold black breast-band; yellow belly.
(Konkoit) 20 cm

RED-HEADED WEAVER (male)
Woodland. Red head, mantle and breast;
pink bill; belly white.
(Rooikopwewer) 15 cm

SCARLET-CHESTED SUNBIRD (male)
Woodland. Black with scarlet throat
and breast; green forehead.
(Rooikeelsuikerbekkie) 13-15 cm

MARICO SUNBIRD (male)
Bushveld. Claret-red lower breast-
band; black belly; above head and
breast glossy-green.
(Maricosuikerbekkie) 13-14 cm

RED-SHOULDERED WIDOW (male)
Wetlands. Entirely black except for red
shoulder-patch; whitish bill.
(Kortstertflap) 19 cm

RED-HEADED QUELEA (male)
Grasslands. Red head on small,
buffy seed-eater.
(Rooikopkwelea) 11,5 cm

red plumage **123**

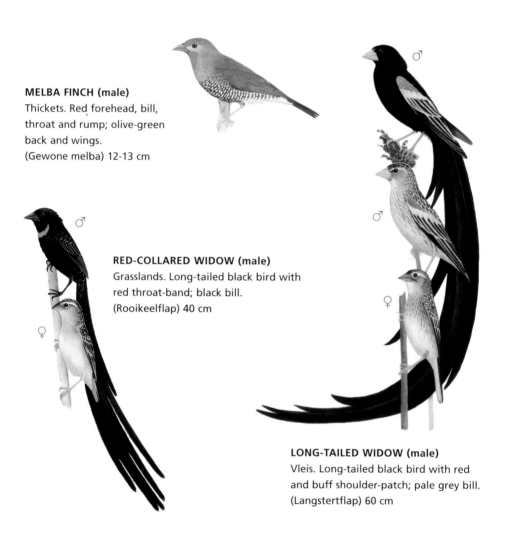

MELBA FINCH (male)
Thickets. Red forehead, bill, throat and rump; olive-green back and wings.
(Gewone melba) 12-13 cm

RED-COLLARED WIDOW (male)
Grasslands. Long-tailed black bird with red throat-band; black bill.
(Rooikeelflap) 40 cm

LONG-TAILED WIDOW (male)
Vleis. Long-tailed black bird with red and buff shoulder-patch; pale grey bill.
(Langstertflap) 60 cm

FIRE-CROWNED BISHOP (male)
Wetlands. Red above, plus red upper breast and vent; rest black, including wings.
(Vuurkopvink) 15 cm

RED BISHOP (male)
Wetlands. Red above, on upper breast and vent; front and below black; wings brown.
(Rooivink) 14 cm

BROWN FIREFINCH (male)
Thickets. Reddish mask, throat and
breast; rest grey-brown.
(Bruinvuurvinkie) 10 cm

GOLDEN-BACKED PYTILIA (male)
Thickets. Red forehead, bill, throat, rump
and upper tail; olive-green back; orange-
edged wings.
(Geelrugmelba) 11 cm

RED-FACED CRIMSON-WING (male)
Thickets. Red mask, upperparts and rear
flanks; dark below.
(Rooirugsaadvretertjie) 12 cm

NYASA SEEDCRACKER
Woodland. Red head from central crown;
red throat and breast; red rump and
upper tail; rest brown.
(Rooistertsaadvretertjie) 13 cm

RED-BILLED FIREFINCH
Bushveld. Red head, neck, breast and upper
tail coverts in male; red lores and upper tail
in female; rest of body grey-brown.
(Rooibekvuurvinkie) 10 cm

BLUE-BILLED FIREFINCH
Bushveld. Face, throat, breast, flanks
and rump red; above, including
crown, grey-brown; bill blue-black.
(Kaapse vuurvinkie) 11 cm

JAMESON'S FIREFINCH
Bushveld. Head, underparts and rump
pinkish-red; upperparts brown
washed pinkish-red; bill blue-black.
(Jamesonse vuurvinkie) 11 cm

RED-THROATED TWINSPOT (male)
Dense bush. Red head (not crown),
throat breast and rump. Below black
with white spots.
(Rooikeelkolpensie) 12,5 cm

ORANGE-BREASTED WAXBILL (male)
Wetlands, cultivations. Red mask, bill and
vent; yellow underparts.
(Rooiassie) 9 cm

GREEN TWINSPOT (male)
Forest fringes. Small green bird with red
face; black below spotted white.
(Groenkolpensie) 10 cm

COMMON WAXBILL
Wetlands. Red mask, bill and central
belly; brown-barred below.
(Rooibeksysie) 13 cm

BLACK-CHEEKED WAXBILL
Thornveld. Rump and underparts deep wine-red; bill and mask black.
(Swartwangsysie) 12-13 cm

GREY WAXBILL
Bushveld. Small grey bird with red rump and upper tail coverts; red eyes and black bill.
(Gryssysie) 11 cm

SWEE WAXBILL
Thick bush. Red back and upper tail coverts; red and black bill.
(Suidelike swie) 9-10 cm

CUT-THROAT FINCH (male)
Woodland. Speckled bird with broad red throat-band; white bill.
(Bandkeelvink) 12 cm

RED-HEADED FINCH (male)
Thornveld. Red head; grey-brown above; speckled below; heavy bill.
(Rooikopvink) 13 cm

birds with red bill,

T he title of this chapter refers to those parts of a bird that include any bare skin encircling the eyes (the orbital ring or eye-ring), bare flesh on the face or throat, its beak or bill, and its legs. Collectively these parts of a bird are called its 'soft parts' or 'bare parts' – in other words, any part of the body that is not covered by feathers. Many birds have brightly coloured bills or legs, often both, and among the larger species we frequently see bare skin around the bird's face or neck.

All too often, especially when a bird sighting is brief, we can only recall the colours of its soft parts once it has flown out of sight, and it is just this situation that this chapter caters for.

*African
Spoonbill*

THE CERE

At the base of the upper mandible of birds of prey, some parrots and some pigeons, there is a soft, swollen region called the cere. It is usually unfeathered, except in certain parrots. In pigeons it appears as two fleshy swellings above the nostrils, as seen in the common Feral Pigeon. The colouring of the cere may be grey, yellow (as in many birds of prey), orange or red according to the species, but its exact function is unknown.

In many birds of prey the lores, the region between the base of the bill and the eye, is bare of feathers and may be coloured red, yellow or grey. This unfeathered region probably functions as an aid to cleanliness, especially in those raptors that feed on messy food items. In the Gymnogene or Harrier-hawk the entire face and forward section of the head is bare. In many vultures the entire head and much of the neck is unfeathered for the same reason.

facial skin and legs

THE BIRDS YOU WILL FIND IN THIS CHAPTER

HARTLAUB'S GULL
Coastal. Bill and legs deep
red; plumage white and grey.
(Hartlaubse meeu) 38 cm

AFRICAN SKIMMER
Inland waters. Bill and legs
red; plumage dark brown
and white.
(Waterploeër) 38 cm

CASPIAN TERN
Inland and estuarine waters.
Large red bill; legs black; plumage
grey and white.
(Reusesterretjie) 52 cm

GREY-HEADED GULL
Inland and coastal. Bill and
legs bright red; plumage
white and grey.
(Gryskopmeeu) 42 cm

COMMON TERN
Coastal. Red bill with black tip
when breeding; plumage grey
and white; cap black.
(Gewone sterretjie) 35 cm

KELP GULL
Coastal. Large yellow bill with
red spot on lower mandible;
plumage black and white.
(Swartrugmeeu) 60 cm

ARCTIC TERN
Coastal. Red bill when breeding.
Plumage grey and white; cap black.
(Arktiese sterretjie) 35 cm

WHITE STORK
Grasslands, bushveld. Red bill and
legs; plumage black and white.
(Witooievaar) 117 cm

WHISKERED TERN
Inland pans. Red bill and legs
when breeding; plumage grey
and white; cap black.
(Witbaardsterretjie) 23 cm

BLACK STORK
Inland waters. Red bill and legs;
plumage black and white.
(Grootswartooievaar) 122 cm

SADDLE-BILLED STORK
Wetlands. Red and black bill
with yellow saddle; black and
white plumage.
(Saalbekooievaar) 145 cm

YELLOW-BILLED STORK
Wetlands. Red facial skin and
legs; plumage black and white.
(Nimmersat) 97 cm

red bill, facial skin and legs **131**

LESSER FLAMINGO
Saline waters. Bill deep red;
legs red; plumage pink.
(Kleinflamink) 102 cm

AFRICAN FINFOOT
Rivers. Bill and legs red;
plumage brown and white.
(Watertrapper) 63 cm

AFRICAN SPOONBILL: N82
Wetlands. Red bill and legs;
plumage white.
(Lepelaar) 91 cm

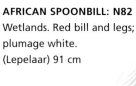

BALD IBIS
Dry grasslands. Red crown and
bill; plumage iridescent blue.
(Kalkoenibis) 71 cm

SPUR-WINGED GOOSE (male)
Wetlands. Red bill and forehead;
pink legs; plumage glossy-green.
(Wildemakou) 102 cm

RED-BILLED TEAL
Wetlands. Red bill; brown cap;
mottled-brown plumage.
(Rooibekeend) 48 cm

PURPLE GALLINULE
Wetlands. Red frontal shield
and bill; pink legs; plumage
glossy-green and blue.
(Grootkoningriethaan) 46 cm

RED-KNOBBED COOT
Wetlands. Red knobs on head;
red eyes; white frontal shield
and bill; black plumage.
(Bleshoender) 43 cm

LESSER GALLINULE
Wetlands. Red bill and dark red
legs; plumage glossy blue-green.
(Kleinkoningriethaan) 25 cm

red bill, facial skin and legs **133**

LESSER MOORHEN
Wetlands. Red on frontal shield
and culmen; yellow bill; pink legs;
blackish plumage.
(Kleinwaterhoender) 23 cm

LONG-TOED PLOVER
Floodpans, backwaters. Red bill
with black tip; red eye-ring and
legs; black and white body.
(Witvlerkkiewiet) 30 cm

BLACK CRAKE
Wetlands. Black bird with
red legs; yellow bill.
(Swartriethaan) 20-23 cm

CROWNED PLOVER
Dry veld. Black-tipped red bill
and red legs; white ring around
black cap.
(Kroonkiewiet) 30 cm

THREE-BANDED PLOVER
Wetlands. Red bill and eye-ring;
white below with two black
chest-bands.
(Driebandstrandkiewiet) 18 cm

WATTLED CRANE
Wetlands. Large crane
with a fleshy red base to
its bill; grey above;
white below.
(Lelkraanvoël) 120 cm

AFRICAN BLACK OYSTERCATCHER
Rocky coasts. Black bird with red bill,
eye-ring and legs.
(Swarttobie) 51 cm

BLACK-WINGED STILT
Wetlands. Long red legs; white
body; black bill and wings.
(Rooipootelsie) 38 cm

CRESTED FRANCOLIN
Bushveld. A bantam-like
francolin with red legs.
(Bospatrys) 32 cm

RED-BILLED FRANCOLIN
Dry woodland. Red bill and legs;
yellow eye-ring.
(Rooibekfisant) 30-38 cm

BLACK KORHAAN
Red bill on mostly black bird;
pale yellow legs; buffy above.
(Swartkorhaan) 53 cm

RED-NECKED FRANCOLIN
Coastal bush. Red bill, facial and throat skin and legs; plumage variable, may have white about head.
(Rooikeelfisant) 32-44 cm

SWAINSON'S FRANCOLIN
Bushveld. Black tip to red bill; red facial and throat skin; legs black; plumage dark brown.
(Bosveldfisant) 34-39 cm

NATAL FRANCOLIN
Koppies, riverbanks. Red and yellow bill; red legs; speckled below.
(Natalse fisant) 30-38 cm

HELMETED GUINEAFOWL
Bushveld. Red crown on blue head; red wattle-tips.
(Gewone tarentaal) 53-58 cm

HOODED VULTURE
Game regions. Reddish facial and neck skin; slender white bill; brown and white plumage.
(Monnikaasvoël) 70 cm

WHITE-HEADED VULTURE
Game regions. Red tip to pale blue bill; pink facial and neck skin; pink legs; white and brown plumage. (Witkopaasvoël) 85 cm

GABAR GOSHAWK
Woodland. Small grey raptor with red cere and legs. (Witkruissperwer) 30-34 cm

DARK CHANTING GOSHAWK
Woodland. Grey raptor with coral-red legs and pink cere. (Donkersingvalk) 50-56 cm

LAPPET-FACED VULTURE
Game regions. Scarlet-red facial and neck skin; plumage brown and white. (Swartaasvoël) 115 cm

BATELEUR
Game regions. Red bill and facial skin; red legs; plumage mostly black; tawny wings; short tail. (Berghaan) 55-70 cm

**EASTERN RED-FOOTED KESTREL
(male)**
Grasslands. Small, pale grey
raptor with red cere, eye-ring
and legs.
(Oostelike rooipootvalk) 28-30 cm

**WESTERN RED-FOOTED KESTREL
(male)**
Grasslands. Small, dark grey raptor
with red cere, eye-ring and legs.
(Westelike rooipootvalk)
28-30 cm

NAMAQUA DOVE (male)
Dry veld. Red bill with yellow tip;
red legs; black forehead, throat and
breast; long tail.
(Namakwaduifie) 27 cm

RED-EYED DOVE
Wooded regions. Red eye-ring around
red eyes; wide black collar; grey crown;
grey-pink underparts.
(Grootringduif) 33-36 cm

AFRICAN MOURNING DOVE
Riverine woodland. Red eye-ring
around yellow eyes; red legs; grey
head; black collar; pink breast.
(Rooioogtortelduif) 30 cm

KNYSNA LOURIE
Forests. Red bill and eye-ring on green bird with crested head. (Knysnaloerie) 47 cm

GREEN PIGEON
Riverine woodland. Red bill with white tip; red legs; white eye; green upperparts. (Papegaaiduif) 30 cm

PURPLE-CRESTED LOURIE
Red eye-ring on green head with purple crest. (Bloukuifloerie) 47 cm

ROCK PIGEON
Cliffs. Red mask; yellow eye; red legs; upperparts dull red, spotted white. (Kransduif) 33 cm

LILIAN'S LOVEBIRD
Zambezi Valley. Red bill on rose-red head; whitish eye-ring; rest green. (Niassaparkiet) 17-18 cm

DIEDERIK CUCKOO
Wooded habitats. Red eye-rings on glossy-green cuckoo; juvenile has pinkish-red bill and no eye-ring. (Diederikkie) 18,5 cm

RED-FACED MOUSEBIRD
Woodland, suburbia. Red facial
mask and legs on long-tailed,
brownish bird with crest.
(Rooiwangmuisvoël) 32-34 cm

BROWN-HOODED KINGFISHER
Woodland. Red bill on brown-streaked
head and body; red legs; black and blue
wings and tail.
(Bruinkopvisvanger) 23-24 cm

PYGMY KINGFISHER
Woodland. Red bill and legs on small
kingfisher; blue above; sandy below;
mauve sides to head.
(Dwergvisvanger) 13 cm

WOODLAND KINGFISHER
Woodland. Blue and white; bill red above,
black below; juvenile has all-red bill.
(Bosveldvisvanger) 23-24 cm

GREY-HOODED KINGFISHER
Woodland. Red, dagger-like bill
on grey head; red legs.
(Gryskopvisvanger) 20 cm

MALACHITE KINGFISHER
Streams. Red bill and legs on small
kingfisher; glossy-blue above;
orange-buff below.
(Kuifkopvisvanger) 14 cm

RED-BILLED WOOD HOOPOE
Curved red bill; red legs on long-tailed, glossy blue-green bird.
(Gewone kakelaar) 30-36 cm

MONTEIRO'S HORNBILL
Red bill with white base; dark head and breast; dark upperparts; white below.
(Monteirose neushoringvoël) 54-58 cm

RED-BILLED HORNBILL
Woodland. Prominent red bill on black and white hornbill; upperparts speckled white.
(Rooibekneushoringvoël) 42-50 cm

CROWNED HORNBILL
Lowland forests. Prominent red bill with yellow base; dark brown above; white below.
(Gekroonde neushoringvoël) 50-57 cm

GROUND HORNBILL
Woodland. Large black, terrestrial bird with red facial and throat skin.
(Bromvoël) 90 cm

EUROPEAN GOLDEN ORIOLE
Woodland. Coral-red bill on yellow
bird with black wings.
(Europese wielewaal) 24 cm

BUSH BLACKCAP
Hillside scrub. Red bill on greyish bird
with black cap; orange legs.
(Rooibektiptol) 17 cm

AFRICAN GOLDEN ORIOLE
Woodland. Coral-red bill on yellow
bird with black mask.
(Afrikaanse wielewaal) 24 cm

RED-EYED BULBUL
Semi-arid bush. Yellow-vented bulbul
with red eye-ring on black head.
(Rooioogtiptol) 19-21 cm

BLACK-HEADED ORIOLE
Woodland. Coral-red bill on yellow
bird with black head.
(Swartkopwielewaal) 25 cm

WATTLE-EYED FLYCATCHER
Riverine thickets. Small, black-and-
white bird with red eye-wattles;
whitish eyes.
(Beloogbosbontrokkie) 12 cm

YELLOW-BILLED OXPECKER
Game regions. Red-tipped yellow bill
on brown bird.
(Geelbekrenostervoël) 22 cm

RED-BILLED BUFFALO WEAVER
Woodland. Stout red bill on blackish
weaver.
(Buffelwewer) 24 cm

RED-BILLED HELMET SHRIKE
Riverine forests. Black bird with red bill,
eye-wattles and legs; white vent.
(Swarthelmlaksman) 22 cm

RED-BILLED OXPECKER
Game regions. Red bill; red eye with
yellow eye-wattle on brown bird.
(Rooibekrenostervoël) 20-22 cm

red bill, facial skin and legs **143**

GOLDEN-BACKED PYTILIA
Thornveld thickets. Red bill on grey head;
golden-orange wings.
(Geelrugmelba) 11 cm

RED-BILLED QUELEA
Croplands. Red or pinkish bill on
small, weaver-type bird; male has
blackish face.
(Rooibekkwelea) 13 cm

QUAIL FINCH
Grassveld. Very small finch; male has
red bill; female has red and black bill;
banded breast.
(Gewone kwartelvinkie) 9,5 cm

RED-HEADED WEAVER (male)
Woodland. Coral-red bill on weaver
with red head, mantle and breast.
(Rooikopwewer) 15 cm

MELBA FINCH
Thornveld thickets. Red bill on grey head;
male with red forehead and throat; male
and female banded below.
(Gewone melba) 12-13 cm

ORANGE-BREASTED WAXBILL
Wetlands. Red bill; grey above; yellow below with banded flanks.
(Rooiassie) 8,5-9 cm

PIN-TAILED WHYDAH (male)
Suburbia and general. Black-and-white, long-tailed bird with red bill.
(Koningrooibekkie) 34 cm

COMMON WAXBILL
Reedbeds. Red-billed waxbill with red mask and underbelly.
(Rooibeksysie) 13 cm

SHAFT-TAILED WHYDAH
Thornveld. Red bill and legs; black above; buffy below; very long tail-shafts.
(Pylstertrooibekkie) 34 cm

STEEL-BLUE WIDOW FINCH (male)
Mixed bush. Small, black bird with red bill and legs.
(Staalblouvinkie) 11 cm

VIOLET-EARED WAXBILL
Dry thornveld. Red-billed waxbill with longish tail; violet cheeks.
(Koningblousysie) 13-15 cm

There are 32 southern African birds with partly orange plumage or soft parts, especially beaks and legs. Orange as a plumage colour is particularly attractive since it is often set against a yellow background, as seen, for example, in the beautiful Orange-breasted Bush Shrike. Like certain other bright colours, orange probably has an important signalling function in species recognition, and perhaps courtship or pair-bonding rituals, as suggested by the fact that the orange colour most often occurs on the bird's breast, forehead or bill, where it is most easily seen by others.

Natal Robin

PELLETS

Many birds regurgitate undigested food items in the shape of oval or round pellets. The action involves a series of convulsive movements of the extended head and neck with the bill open. In owls, which swallow prey whole, the pellet consists mainly of fur and small mammal bones. In kingfishers, herons and other fish-eaters, the pellets contain fish bones, scales and similar hard materials. Even shrikes, rollers and others that prey on large insects and small reptiles will regurgitate such indigestible items as beetle carapaces, claws and small bones. The disection and examination of bird pellets therefore provides an insight to the bird's preferred diet.

orange plumage

THE BIRDS YOU WILL FIND IN THIS CHAPTER

Pygmy Goose

Br.

Non-br.

LESSER CRESTED TERN
Coastal. Orange bill only. Black or
partially black cap; grey above;
white below with black legs.
(Kuifkopsterretjie) 40 cm

RUDDY TURNSTONE (breeding)
Shorelines. Orange legs; black bill;
head and below white; black facial marks
and breast-band; rufous wings.
(Steenloper) 22 cm

PYGMY GOOSE
Quiet waters. Orange bill and
orange-buff underparts in both
sexes; upperparts dark green.
(Dwerggans) 33 cm

WHITE-FACED OWL
Woodland. Deep orange
eyes in white facial disc
with black border;
plumage grey.
(Witwanguil) 25-28 cm

RINGED PLOVER
Shorelines. Black-tipped
orange bill and orange legs;
bold black breast-band on
white underparts.
(Ringnekstrandkiewiet) 18 cm

CAPE EAGLE OWL
Rocky valleys. Orange eyes in
immature; orange-yellow in
adult. Large 'eared' owl; dark
above; blotched dark below.
(Kaapse ooruil) 48-55 cm

LESSER STRIPED SWALLOW
Lowveld. Cap, ear coverts and rump rich orange; below white, well streaked black.
(Kleinstreepswael) 16 cm

MALACHITE KINGFISHER
Ponds. Orange-buff below; blue above; bill and legs red.
(Kuifkopvisvanger) 14 cm

GREATER STRIPED SWALLOW
Highveld. Orange cap and pale orange rump; whitish below, lightly streaked black.
(Grootstreepswael) 20 cm

HALF-COLLARED KINGFISHER
Quiet rivers. Orange wash on belly and vent; throat white; above blue; bill black; legs red.
(Blouvisvanger) 20 cm

WIRE-TAILED SWALLOW
Lowveld rivers. Orange cap; black mask; white below with fine tail-streamers.
(Draadstertswael) 13 cm

ORANGE THRUSH
Forests. Rich orange throat, breast and flanks; white belly and vent; double white wing-bar. (Oranjelyster) 23 cm

BRADFIELD'S HORNBILL
Woodland. Distinctive orange bill on brown upperparts; bill-base and eyes pale yellow. (Bradfieldse neushoringvoël) 50-57 cm

YELLOW-FRONTED TINKER BARBET
Woodland. Yellow forehead normally looks orange; above black, speckled white and yellow; below pale yellow. (Geelblestinker) 12 cm

KURRICHANE THRUSH
Woodland. Orange bill, eye-ring, legs and flanks; white belly; black moustachial streaks. (Rooibeklyster) 22 cm

OLIVE THRUSH
Forests and suburbia. Orange bill and belly; orange-yellow legs; speckled throat. (Olyflyster) 24 cm

ORANGE-THROATED LONGCLAW
Grasslands. Orange throat with black border; underparts yellow; above grey-brown. (Oranjekeelkalkoentjie) 20 cm

SHORT-TOED ROCK THRUSH
Rocky hills. Orange below with white throat; above grey-brown with orange rump. Male has grey throat and mantle, white cap; breast to vent rich orange.
(Korttoonkliplyster) 18 cm

SENTINEL ROCK THRUSH
Rocky hills. Orange rump and outer tail feathers; light orange wash to underparts; breast speckled. Male has dull grey head, breast and mantle; orange lower breast to vent.
(Langtoonkliplyster) 21 cm

CAPE ROBIN
Forest fringes and gardens. Orange breast, rump, upper tail coverts and tail fringes; white eyebrows; underbody grey-buff.
(Gewone janfrederik) 18 cm

WHITE-THROATED ROBIN
Thickets. Grey, black and white above; below white chin to lower breast; flanks and belly washed orange.
(Witkeeljanfrederik) 16-18 cm

ORANGE-BREASTED ROCKJUMPER (male)
Rocky grasslands. Rump and upper tail coverts orange; below orange lower breast; paler towards belly.
(Oranjeborsberglyster) 21 cm

orange plumage **151**

HEUGLIN'S ROBIN
Thickets. Underparts entirely rich orange
extending to rump and tail fringes; white
eyebrows on black hood.
(Heuglinse janfrederik) 19-20 cm

CHORISTER ROBIN
Forests. Underparts entirely orange; hood
black; wings and upper tail dark grey.
(Lawaaimakerjanfrederik) 20 cm

LIVINGSTONE'S FLYCATCHER
Riverine forests. Grey head; yellow under-
parts; orange upper tail with black band.
(Rooistertvlieëvanger) 12 cm

NATAL ROBIN
Forests. Entirely orange except for
brownish crown and silver-grey wings.
(Nataljanfrederik)
18-20 cm

ORANGE-BREASTED BUSH SHRIKE
Bushveld. Grey cap and mantle; olive-green
wings and upper tail; below yellow with
orange breast-patch.
(Oranjeborsboslaksman) 18-19 cm

ORANGE-BREASTED SUNBIRD (male)
Fynbos. Head and throat glossy-green;
breast-band purple; breast orange grading
to yellow at vent; tail longish.
(Oranjeborssuikerbekkie) 15 cm

BLACK-FRONTED BUSH SHRIKE
Forests. Chin to underbelly rich orange;
vent yellow; above olive-green; cap grey.
(Swartoogboslaksman) 19 cm

ORANGE-BREASTED WAXBILL
Reedbeds. Small waxbill with red
bill and mask; below yellow with
orange wash on breast; orange vent;
banded flanks.
(Rooiassie) 8,5-9 cm

GOLDEN-BREASTED BUNTING
Bushveld. Head black with white stripes;
chin to lower breast yellow, with orange
wash on breast; vent white.
(Rooirugstreepkoppie) 16 cm

GREY-HEADED BUSH SHRIKE
Riverine forests. Yellow chin to vent, except
for orange breast; head grey; rest olive-
green; eyes orange-yellow; heavy bill black.
(Spookvoël) 25-27 cm

birds with

O f all the bright colours seen in birds, yellow is probably the most common. In the majority of birds with yellow plumage it is their underparts that carry this colour, many being yellow from chin to tail. Other birds have white underparts, or some light colour such as cream, buff or beige, and this arrangement of pale underparts serves a purpose known as counter-shading. A bird receives most sunlight on its darker upperparts, while its pale underparts are in shade. The contrast between the dark upper surface and pale undersurface is thereby reduced so that the bird does not stand out from its background. For example, a bird that is olive-green above and yellow below will tend to appear the same colour all over since its shaded yellow underparts will take on a greenish appearance.

In this chapter only true yellow, a colour likely to make a lasting impression on an observer is included. Waterbirds that are identifiable by their yellow bills or legs are included, but not the many birds of prey that have yellow ceres and legs, since these cannot be regarded as specific identification features.

*Yellow
White-eye*

THE WARBLERS
This is a somewhat ambiguous term used to describe a host of small songbirds belonging to various groups found in both temperate and tropical regions. In southern Africa the term is used in particular for the many small European birds that migrate over very long distances to spend their non-breeding months (our summer) in the sub-tropics, namely the Palearctic Warblers. In general terms, the warblers also include the apalises, penduline tits, eremomelas, crombecs, grass warblers (cisticolas), prinias and titbabblers. The Palearctic warblers, frequently referred to as just LBJs, are among the more difficult little brown birds to identify unless one is familiar with their habitats and songs.

yellow colouring

THE BIRDS YOU WILL FIND IN THIS CHAPTER

PINK-BACKED PELICAN
Inland and coastal.
Yellow bill-pouch and feet.
(Kleinpelikaan) 135 cm

CAPE GANNET
Coastal. This mostly white seabird
has a distinctive yellow wash over
its head and hind neck.
(Witmalgas) 84-94 cm

EASTERN WHITE PELICAN
Inland and coastal. When breeding
it has a yellow bill-pouch and
yellow patch on its upper breast;
legs are pinkish.
(Witpelikaan) 180 cm

KELP GULL
Coastal. Black-and-white gull
with yellow bill and a red
spot on the lower mandible.
(Swartrugmeeu) 60 cm

SWIFT TERN
Coastal. A fairly large tern
with a yellow bill.
(Geelbeksterretjie) 50 cm

BLACK EGRET
Wetlands. A blackish egret
with yellow feet.
(Swartreier) 66 cm

GREAT WHITE HERON
Wetlands. A large heron.
When not breeding it has a
yellow bill and black legs.
(Grootwitreier) 95 cm

SADDLE-BILLED STORK
Wetlands. Huge pied stork
with large red and black bill,
and a yellow 'saddle' on the
upper mandible.
(Saalbekooievaar) 145 cm

LITTLE EGRET
Wetlands. A white egret with
yellow feet and black legs.
(Kleinwitreier) 64 cm

INTERMEDIATE EGRET
Wetlands. A medium-size, robust
white egret with a yellow bill.
(Geelbekwitreier) 68 cm

YELLOW-BILLED STORK
Wetlands. Yellow, slightly curved
bill on white stork with red face
and legs.
(Nimmersat) 97 cm

WATTLED PLOVER
Wetlands. Yellow bill with black tip; yellow wattles and legs; entire breast greyish. (Lelkiewiet) 35 cm

YELLOW-BILLED DUCK
Wetlands. The only duck with a distinctive yellow bill with a black saddle. (Geelbekeend) 53-58 cm

BLACK CRAKE
Wetlands. Small black waterbird with yellow bill; red legs. (Swartriethaan) 20-23 cm

RUDDY TURNSTONE
Coastal. In non-breeding plumage has yellow legs. (Steenloper) 22 cm

WHITE-CROWNED PLOVER
Wetlands. Yellow bill with black tip; long yellow wattles and yellow legs; underparts white. (Witkopkiewiet) 30 cm

YELLOW-BILLED KITE
Aerial. Brown kite with forked tail; yellow bill, cere and legs.
(Geelbekwou) 55 cm

EMERALD CUCKOO
Forests. The only green cuckoo with a yellow belly.
(Mooimeisie) 20 cm

GREEN COUCAL
Coastal forests. A dull green coucal with a yellow bill.
(Groenvleiloerie) 23 cm

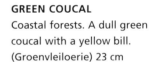

MEYER'S PARROT
Woodland. Small, brown-headed parrot with yellow forehead and shoulders; green belly; pale blue back.
(Bosveldpapegaai) 23 cm

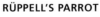

RÜPPELL'S PARROT
Woodland. Small, dark brown parrot with yellow shoulders and underwing coverts; deep-blue belly; female with deep-blue belly and back.
(Bloupenspapegaai) 23 cm

SWALLOW-TAILED BEE-EATER
Kalahari woodland. Blue and green bee-eater with forked tail and yellow throat.
(Swaelstertbyvreter) 20-22 cm

BROAD-BILLED ROLLER
Palm woodland. The only yellow-billed roller.
(Geelbektroupant) 27 cm

LITTLE BEE-EATER
Woodland. Small bee-eater with yellow throat, black upper breast patch and orange-buff underparts.
(Kleinbyvreter) 17 cm

SOUTHERN YELLOW-BILLED HORNBILL
Woodland. Pied hornbill with a prominent yellow bill.
(Geelbekneushoringvoël) 48-60 cm

EUROPEAN BEE-EATER
Wooded regions. Yellow throat; blue forehead and underparts.
(Europese byvreter) 25-29 cm

GOLDEN-RUMPED TINKER BARBET
Forests. Black above with yellow wing
edges and rump; whitish below with
yellow belly.
(Swartblestinker) 10 cm

YELLOW-FRONTED TINKER BARBET
Woodland. Black and white above with
yellow wing-feather edges; orange
forehead; pale yellow below.
(Geelblestinker) 12 cm

PIED BARBET
Woodland. Red forehead; yellow eyebrows
and edges to wing and tail feathers.
(Bonthoutkapper) 17-18 cm

RED-FRONTED TINKER BARBET
Lowland forests. Black-and-white above
with yellow wing-feather edges; red
forehead; pale yellow below.
(Rooiblestinker) 10,5 cm

CRESTED BARBET
Woodland. Bill pale yellow; head and
underparts yellow with red spotting;
above black with white feather edges.
(Kuifkophoutkapper) 23 cm

GREATER HONEYGUIDE (immature)
Woodland. The young bird is brown above and yellow below, grading to paler at vent. (Grootheuningwyser) 19-20 cm

YELLOW-THROATED LONGCLAW
Open woodland. Above eyebrows and feather edges yellow; below yellow with black gorget.
(Geelkeelkalkoentjie) 20 cm

YELLOW-BREASTED PIPIT
Montane grassland. Below entirely yellow, including underwing coverts; duller in winter. (Geelborskoester) 16-18 cm

ORANGE-THROATED LONGCLAW
Grasslands. Eyebrows and below yellow; throat orange bordered black.
(Oranjekeelkalkoentjie) 20 cm

YELLOW WAGTAIL
Wetlands. Below yellow; above green-grey; various head patterns.
(Geelkwikkie) 18 cm

BLACK CUCKOOSHRIKE (female)
Woodland. Dull olive-brown above with
yellow wing-feathers and tail edges;
below banded black on white.
(Swartkatakoeroe) 22 cm

EUROPEAN GOLDEN ORIOLE
Woodland. Entirely yellow except for black
wings, tail feathers and lores; bill pink.
(Europese wielewaal) 24 cm

BLACK-HEADED ORIOLE
Woodland. Black head and throat;
pink bill; rest yellow except black
primaries; green upper tail.
(Swartkopwielewaal) 25 cm

AFRICAN GOLDEN ORIOLE
Woodland. Entirely yellow except for
black mask, primaries and central tail
feathers; female greener; bill pink.
(Afrikaanse wielewaal)
24 cm

YELLOW-SPOTTED NICATOR
Dense bush. Greenish above; wing
feathers and tail tipped yellow;
underbelly, thighs and vent yellow.
(Geelvleknikator) 23 cm

yellow colouring 163

YELLOW-BELLIED BULBUL
Riverine forests. Below (including
underwings) yellow; head grey;
rest olive-brown.
(Geelborswillie) 20-23 cm

CAPE BULBUL
Coastal bush. Dark brown
head and breast; white
eye-rings; yellow vent.
(Kaapse tiptol) 21 cm

BLACK-EYED BULBUL
Woodland and gardens. Black eyes
and tufted head; yellow vent.
(Swartoogtiptol) 20-22 cm

RED-EYED BULBUL
Woodland and gardens. Black tufted
head; red eye-rings; yellow vent.
(Rooioogtiptol) 21 cm

STARRED ROBIN
Forests. Underparts yellow; head
grey; rest deep olive-green.
(Witkoljanfrederik) 15-16 cm

ICTERINE WARBLER
Acacia thornveld. Brown above with yellow flight-feather edges; below yellow.
(Spotvoël) 14-15 cm

YELLOW-BREASTED APALIS
Bushveld. Yellow-green above; some grey on head; yellow breast; white throat and belly; small central breast-bar often absent.
(Geelborskleinjantjie) 10-12,5 cm

YELLOW WARBLER
Reeds and forest fringes. Yellow below; above olive-brown; wing feathers and tail edged yellow.
(Geelsanger)
14-15 cm

CAPE PENDULINE TIT
Woodland. Very small size; forehead blackish; throat white; rest of underparts yellow.
(Kaapse kapokvoël) 9-10 cm

BAR-THROATED APALIS
Woodland. The northern race is yellow below the black breast-band; throat white; above greyish; eyes whitish.
(Bandkeelkleinjantjie) 12-13 cm

YELLOW-BELLIED EREMOMELA
Bushveld. Yellow belly on small, greyish bird; paler on breast; darker above; tail short. (Geelpensbossanger) 9-10 cm

SAFFRON PRINIA
Forest fringes. Eyebrows and below saffron-yellow; above brown; tail long. (Gevlekte langstertjie) 14 cm

GREEN-CAPPED EREMOMELA
Woodland. Olive-green above; pale eyes with red eye-rings; yellow breast; white chin and underbelly. (Donkerwangbossanger) 12 cm

MASHONA HYLIOTA
Woodland. Blackish above with white wing-patch; washed yellow below, strongest on breast. (Mashonahyliota) 14 cm

YELLOW-THROATED WARBLER
Forests. Olive-green above. Chestnut cap; eyebrows and breast yellow; belly white. (Geelkeelsanger) 11 cm

LIVINGSTONE'S FLYCATCHER
Riverine forests. Grey cap; olive-green wings; rufous upper tail; yellow underparts.
(Rooistertvlieëvanger)12 cm

BOKMAKIERIE
Bush and suburbia. Above grey cap and mantle; rest olive-green; yellow below with black gorget.
(Bokmakierie) 23 cm

GORGEOUS BUSH SHRIKE
Dense bush. Red throat; black gorget; yellow belly with orange wash; above olive-green; yellow eyebrows.
(Konkoit) 20 cm

ORANGE-BREASTED BUSH SHRIKE
Woodland. Yellow eyebrows and underparts; orange breast; above grey and olive-green.
(Oranjeborsboslaksman) 18-19 cm

GREY-HEADED BUSH SHRIKE
Bushveld. Heavy bill; yellowish eyes; grey hood; rest olive-green; throat and underbelly yellow; breast orange.
(Spookvoël) 25-27 cm

COLLARED SUNBIRD
Riverine woodland. Male has glossy-green upperparts, head and breast; lower breast to vent yellow; female entirely yellow below, duller. (Kortbeksuikerbekkie) 10 cm

YELLOW-BELLIED SUNBIRD (male)
Riverine forests and bush. Head and above glossy-green; breast violet; belly yellow. (Geelpenssuikerbekkie) 11 cm

YELLOW WHITE-EYE
Woodland. Above yellow-green; below entirely clear yellow. (Geelglasogie) 10,5 cm

FOREST WEAVER
Forests. Yellow below; dark brown above; whitish bill and legs. (Bosmusikant) 16 cm

CAPE WHITE-EYE
Woodland and gardens. Various races but all with underlying yellow plumage; greener above. (Kaapse glasogie) 12 cm

CAPE WEAVER
General. Male yellow all over; darker above; orange wash over head and throat; pale eyes. Female paler; yellow wash over head and breast; eyes dark; belly white. (Kaapse wewer) 16-18 cm

BROWN-THROATED WEAVER
Wetlands. All-yellow; male has brown throat-patch; black bill. Female greener above; white belly; bill horn-coloured. (Bruinkeelwewer) 15 cm

YELLOW WEAVER
Wetlands. Both sexes all-yellow; bill dark. (Geelwewer) 16 cm

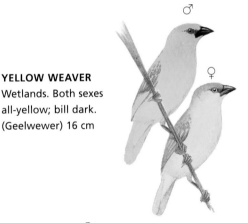

GOLDEN WEAVER
Wetlands. Large yellow weaver; greener above; eyes pale yellow; bill black; male with orange throat in NW regions. (Goudwewer) 18 cm

SPECTACLED WEAVER
Wetlands. All-yellow; wings darker; head with orange wash; bill and eye-stripe black; male with black bib; eyes pale. (Brilwewer) 15-16 cm

MASKED WEAVER

Wetlands and gardens. Breeding male yellow with black mask from forehead to throat; black bill; red eyes. Female greener above, whitish below with yellow wash on breast. (Swartkeelgeelvink) 15 cm

RED-HEADED WEAVER (female)

Woodland. White below with yellowish head; orange-pink bill; yellow feather edges to dark wings. (Rooikopwewer) 15 cm

LESSER MASKED WEAVER

Wetlands. Both sexes yellow; greener above; eyes pale yellow. Male has black mask from central crown to throat. (Kleingeelvink) 14 cm

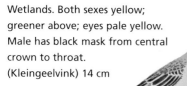

SPOTTED-BACKED WEAVER

Wetlands. Male yellow with dark wings; yellow-speckled mantle; black mask from eyebrows to throat, or entirely black head; bill black; eyes red. Female lacks speckled mantle and mask; throat and breast yellow; belly whitish; eyes red; bill pinkish. (Bontrugwewer) 17 cm

GOLDEN BISHOP (male)

Wetlands. Breeding male has yellow crown, nape and back; below black; bill black; legs pink. (Goudgeelvink) 12 cm

♂

WHITE-WINGED WIDOW (male)
Thornveld and cultivations. Breeding male all-black with yellow and white shoulder-patch; bill pale grey.
(Witvlerkflap) 19 cm

♀

GREEN TWINSPOT (female)
Forest fringes. Small, greenish bird with yellow face and throat; belly black with white spots.
(Groenkolpensie) 10 cm

ORANGE-BREASTED WAXBILL
Reedbeds. Yellow below with barred flanks; male with red mask, breast-patch and vent; above grey-brown.
(Rooiassie) 8,5-9 cm

YELLOW-RUMPED WIDOW (male)
Vleis. Breeding male all-black with yellow rump and shoulder-patch.
(Kaapse flap) 15 cm

♂   ♀

SWEE WAXBILL
Wooded streams. Yellow belly and vent in both sexes; breast whitish; dark green above; red rump and tail coverts; male has black mask.
(Suidelike swie) 9-10 cm

♀

♂

YELLOW-BACKED WIDOW (male)
Marshes. Breeding male all-black with yellow mantle and shoulder-patches.
(Geelrugflap) 22 cm

CUCKOO FINCH

Vleis. Small yellow bird; dark wings
with yellow-edged feathers;
black bill and legs.
(Koekoekvink) 12-13 cm

CAPE CANARY

General. Grey nape and
mantle; rest yellow; greenish
wings with feathers edged
yellow.
(Kaapse kanarie) 13-14 cm

YELLOW-EYED CANARY

Wooded regions. Below yellow;
eyebrows and cheeks yellow;
crown to nape grey; rest greenish
with yellow-edged wing feathers.
(Geeloogkanarie) 12 cm

BULLY CANARY

Woodland. Heavy-billed yellow
canary. Male dark green above and
on breast. Female paler above;
below entirely yellow.
(Dikbekkanarie) 14-15 cm

YELLOW CANARY (male)

Dry bush. Eyebrows, cheeks and
underparts yellow; upperparts
olive-green, paler in W, darkest in SE.
(Geelkanarie) 13-14 cm

WHITE-THROATED CANARY
Karoo. Heavy-billed, greyish canary with yellow rump.
(Witkeelkanarie)
14-15 cm

LEMON-BREASTED CANARY (male)
Bush and grasslands. Yellow breast and rump; belly white; dull greenish above.
(Geelborskanarie) 10 cm

CABANIS'S BUNTING
Miombo woodland. Yellow below; black head with white streaks; back brown with white-edged shoulder feathers.
(Geelstreepkoppie)
15 cm

BLACK-THROATED CANARY
Grassy woodland. Small, greyish canary with blackish throat and yellow rump.
(Bergkanarie) 11-12 cm

GOLDEN-BREASTED BUNTING
Woodland. Yellow below with orange breast; belly and vent white; head black with white streaks; mantle brown with white shoulder-patch.
(Rooirugstreepkoppie)
16 cm

CAPE and DRAKENSBERG SISKINS
Montane scrub. Small, dark canary-like birds with greenish-yellow underparts.
(Kaapse pietjiekanarie)
(Bergpietjiekanarie) 13 cm

birds with

G reen plumage in many birds, from bright greens to dull olive, serve as cryptic colouration within the predominantly green habitat in which they live. Even bright green lovebirds, for example, are very difficult to detect when settled in a leafy tree canopy or feeding in fresh green grass, unless they move. Dull olive-green upperparts, as seen in many small birds, certainly help to render the wearers inconspicuous when seen from above, and this is particularly important for those that forage in the understorey or on the ground. Few waterbirds have green plumage, an exception being the green upperparts of the Pygmy Goose, which lives among floating water lily leaves. Some dabbling ducks have an iridescent green patch on the upperwings called a speculum. The speculum probably functions as an intraspecific visual stimulant or 'advertisement' used by the male bird to establish its status within a flock. This is done frequently when the male bird stands erect and flaps its wings, thereby displaying the colourful speculae.

SUNBIRDS
Sunbirds are the small, brightly iridescent birds with slender, decurved beaks that feed mostly on flower nectar. The bill is adapted to probe into tubular flowers such as those of aloes and ericas. There are many misconceptions about sunbirds, resulting in the local usage of such misleading names as 'honey-sucker' and 'sugarbird', the latter name properly referring to the unrelated genus *Promerops*, the Cape Sugarbird and Gurney's Sugarbird. It is also often assumed that sunbirds are a type of African hummingbird, whereas nothing could be further from the truth. Hummingbirds are found only in the Americas; Africa is the home of sunbirds. Their appearance, food and feeding habits are similar but the two families are quite unrelated. Hummingbirds feed while hovering, with wing-beats of well over four thousand a minute in some species, and can even fly backwards, whereas sunbirds are able to hover only very briefly and must settle to feed.

green plumage

THE BIRDS YOU WILL FIND IN THIS CHAPTER

GLOSSY IBIS
Wetlands. A brown-bronze water-bird with iridescent green wings, long legs and a long curved bill.
(Glansibis) 71 cm

CAPE SHOVELLER
Wetlands. In flight, upperwings show green secondaries separated from blue forewings by a white line.
(Kaapse slopeend) 53 cm

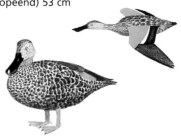

PYGMY GOOSE
Lily pans. Upperparts green; underparts orange-beige; short yellow bill.
(Dwerggans) 33 cm

CAPE TEAL
Wetlands. In flight, upperwings show white secondaries with green central panel. Pale duck with pink bill.
(Teeleend) 46 cm

YELLOW-BILLED DUCK
Wetlands. In flight, upperwings show green secondaries bordered with white. Speckled duck with yellow bill.
(Geelbekeend) 53-58 cm

SPUR-WINGED GOOSE (male)
Wetlands. Upperparts blackish with green iridescence; below white; bill and legs pink.
(Wildemakou) 102 cm

PURPLE GALLINULE
Wetlands. Head and below blue; back, tail and wings green; bill and frontal shield red; legs pink. (Grootkoningriethaan) 46 cm

EMERALD-SPOTTED DOVE
Woodland. Emerald-green spots on the wings; double black bars on the back; rufous flight feathers. (Groenvlekduifie) 20 cm

LESSER GALLINULE
Wetlands. Head and below blue; back, tail and wings green; bill and legs red. (Kleinkoningriethaan) 25 cm

GREEN PIGEON
Riverine woodland. Predominantly green; eyes whitish; bill red and white; legs red; thighs yellow. (Papegaaiduif) 30 cm

FERAL PIGEON
Urban. Many individuals of this variable pigeon have glossy-green neck feathers. (Tuinduif) 33 cm

ROSE-RINGED PARAKEET
Urban. Apple-green parrot with
long tail, red bill and pale eyes.
(Ringnekpapegaai) 40 cm

CAPE PARROT
Forests. Green body and wings;
yellow-brown (or grey) head
and neck; orange-red forehead
and shoulders.
(Grootpapegaai) 35 cm

BROWN-HEADED PARROT
Woodland. Pale green body; dark
green wings; brown head.
(Bruinkoppapegaai) 23 cm

ROSY-FACED LOVEBIRD
Rocky gorges. Rose-red head
with pale bill; green body and
wings; blue back.
(Rooiwangparkiet) 17-18 cm

MEYER'S PARROT
Woodland. Brown head, neck and
wings; blue back and green
underparts; yellow shoulders.
(Bosveldpapegaai) 23 cm

LILIAN'S LOVEBIRD
Zambezi Valley. Rose-red
head with red bill;
rest entirely green.
(Niassaparkiet) 17-18 cm

NARINA TROGON
Forests. Glossy-green head, breast and upperparts; scarlet-red below. Female lacks green breast; bill greenish-yellow. (Bosloerie) 29-34 cm

DIEDERIK CUCKOO
Woodland. Male bright green above; white below; bill black; eyes red. Female similar, but with coppery mantle.
(Diederikkie) 18,5 cm

KNYSNA LOURIE
Forests. Green crested head, nape and underparts; glossy-blue folded wings and tail; red flight feathers. (Knysnaloerie) 47 cm

EMERALD CUCKOO
Forests. Male bright green above, beak to tail, plus breast; belly yellow; eyes dark; beak green. Female brown above; white below with heavy green banding overall. (Mooimeisie) 20 cm

KLAAS'S CUCKOO
Woodland. Male entirely bright green above, bill to tail; white below; eyes dark. Female duller; green above; white below; heavily banded brown; eyes yellow. (Meitjie) 17 cm

green plumage 179

BLUE-CHEEKED BEE-EATER
Wetlands. Entirely green above; pale blue eyebrows, cheeks and belly; chin yellow; throat rufous.
(Blouwangbyvreter) 27-33 cm

SWALLOW-TAILED BEE-EATER
Western savanna. Green above and upper breast; throat yellow with blue band; belly and forked tail blue. Immature apple-green above and below.
(Swaelstertbyvreter) 20-22 cm

LITTLE BEE-EATER
Woodland. Green above; rufous below; yellow throat; black upper breast-patch.
(Kleinbyvreter) 17 cm

OLIVE BEE-EATER
Riverine woodland. Mostly olive-green; cap with brown wash; throat cinnamon.
(Olyfbyvreter) 29-33 cm

WHITE-FRONTED BEE-EATER
Riverine woodland. Back, wings and upper tail green; forehead and chin white; throat red; nape and breast cinnamon; belly to vent blue.
(Rooikeelbyvreter) 22-24 cm

GREEN BARBET
Ngoye Forest. Blackish cap; dull yellow ear-patch; olive-green above; pale olive below.
(Groenhoutkapper) 17 cm

GREEN TINKER BARBET

Coastal forests. Small, dull-green bird with yellow rump and wing feather edges.
(Groentinker) 10 cm

GREEN-HEADED ORIOLE

Montane forests. Green head, back, wings and tail; yellow collar and underparts.
(Groenkopwielewaal) 24 cm

WOODPECKERS

Woodland. Several woodpeckers have dull-green wings, usually with small white or yellow spots. Best identified by their breast and head markings, and their calls.
(Spegte)

Cardinal
Woodpeckers

SOMBRE BULBUL

Forest fringes. In the south, a dull-green bird with whitish eyes; Zambezi and beyond brighter green above, yellow-green below.
(Gewone willie) 19-24 cm

STRIPE-CHEEKED BULBUL

Forest fringes. Overall dull green (yellow-green below); grey cap; white eyelids and cheek-stripes.
(Streepwangwillie) 19-21 cm

RUDD'S APALIS

Coastal bush. Grey cap; olive-green back
and tail; white below with black chest-band.
(Ruddse kleinjantjie) 10,5-12 cm

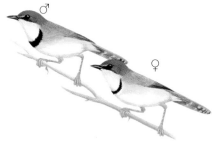

GREEN-BACKED BLEATING WARBLER

Dull olive-green above; white below;
tail usually raised.
(Groenrugkwêkwêvoël) 12 cm

YELLOW-BREASTED APALIS

Bushveld. Grey hood; yellow-green
upperparts; white chin and belly;
yellow breast with small black
breast-bar sometimes present.
(Geelborskleinjantjie) 10-12,5 cm

OLIVE BUSH SHRIKE

Forests. Olive-green above with or without
grey cap (male with black mask); cinnamon
or yellow breast.
(Olyfboslaksman) 17 cm

GREEN-CAPPED EREMOMELA

Woodland. Green cap and mantle;
pale eyes with red eye-rings;
below whitish with yellow breast.
(Donkerwangbossanger) 12 cm

GORGEOUS BUSH SHRIKE

Dense bush. Olive-green above; red throat
and breast with broad black gorget; yellow-
orange belly and vent.
(Konkoit) 20 cm

BOKMAKIERIE
Diverse habitats. Grey cap, nape and mantle; green upperparts; yellow underparts with broad black gorget.
(Bokmakierie) 23 cm

GREY-HEADED BUSH SHRIKE
Riverine bush. Grey hood; yellow eyes; heavy bill; green upperparts; yellow below with broad orange breast.
(Spookvoël) 5-27 cm

LESSER DOUBLE-COLLARED SUNBIRD (male)
Woodlands. Glossy-green head and mantle; blue and narrow red breast-bands, greyish belly.
(Kleinrooibandsuikerbekkie) 12,5 cm

GREATER DOUBLE-COLLARED SUNBIRD (male)
Montane. Glossy-green head and mantle; blue and wide red breast-bands; greyish belly.
(Grootrooibandsuikerbekkie) 14 cm

MALACHITE SUNBIRD (male)
Fynbos. Large, all-green sunbird with a long tail.
(Jangroentjie) 25 cm

Non-br.

♂

♀

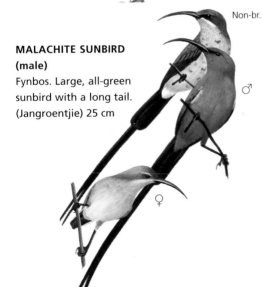

♂

COLLARED SUNBIRD
Riverine forests. Glossy-green upperparts, head and upper breast; rest of underparts yellow. Female has entirely yellow underparts.
(Kortbeksuikerbekkie) 11 cm

green plumage **183**

YELLOW-BELLIED SUNBIRD (male)
Broad-leaved woodland. Glossy blue-green head and mantle; purple breast; yellow belly. (Geelpenssuikerbekkie)
11 cm

ORANGE-BREASTED SUNBIRD (male)
Fynbos. Glossy-green head and mantle; upper breast purple; rest of underparts orange grading to yellow vent; tail extended. (Oranjeborssuikerbekkie) 15 cm

MARICO SUNBIRD (male)
Thornveld. Upperparts, head and breast glossy-green; lower breast with purple and red bands; belly black. (Maricosuikerbekkie) 13-14 cm

OLIVE SUNBIRD (male)
Lowland forests. A large sunbird. Dull olive-green, darker above, paler below. (Olyfsuikerbekkie) 13-15 cm

PURPLE-BANDED SUNBIRD (male)
Coastal bush; forest fringes. A small sunbird with a short bill. Upperparts, head and breast glossy-green; lower breast with purple and red bands; belly black. (Purperbandsuikerbekkie) 11 cm

CAPE WHITE-EYE
Wooded suburbia. Various races: grey to yellow below; yellow-green above; white eye-rings. (Kaapse glasogie) 12 cm

FOREST CANARY
Forest fringes. Olive-green head and upperparts with darker streaks; underparts yellow well streaked with green.
(Gestreepte kanarie) 13 cm

MELBA FINCH
Thorn thickets. Yellow-green mantle and wings; red bill (red forehead and throat in male); red rump and upper tail; banded underparts.
(Gewone melba) 12-13 cm

GREEN TWINSPOT
Forest fringes. Olive-green above (extending to breast in female); yellow face in female; red face and rump in male; belly black with white spots.
(Groenkolpensie) 10 cm

YELLOW CANARY (male)
Dry bush and Karoo scrub. Above light to dark olive-green; eyebrow and underparts yellow.
(Geelkanarie) 13-14 cm

BULLY CANARY
Wooded habitats. Above dark or light olive-green; dark race with olive-green breast; eyebrows and below yellow. Bill thick.
(Dikbekkanarie) 14-15 cm

SWEE WAXBILL
Forest fringes. Dark olive-green back and wings; red lower bill, rump and upper tail coverts; grey cap (male with black mask); below grey-white.
(Suidelike swie) 9-10 cm

birds with **purple,**

To the human eye these colours are certainly pleasing. Their purpose may appear to be purely decorative, but seen through the eyes of a bird they may have a very different function. Research has determined quite recently that many, if not all, birds can see the ultraviolet spectrum, something that is not normally visible to the human eye. The bird's ultraviolet vision may render colours such as purple more brilliant than the human eye can perceive.

♂

*Violet-backed
Sunbird*

BROOD PATCHES

Birds have developed various ways to maintain the temperature of their eggs during incubation. The Emperor Penguin of the Antarctic rests the single egg on its feet and allows the ample folds of its belly-skin to cover them. The Mallee Fowl of Australia deposits its eggs in a self-made compost mound and regulates the internal temperature of the mound by adding or removing compost. However, in the majority of birds, egg-temperature is maintained by transmitting heat from the sitting bird's body. Since one of the primary functions of a bird's plumage is the maintenance of body-heat through insulation, it follows that insufficient heat would normally reach the eggs. This apparent *impasse* is solved by the development of brood patches during the breeding season. These are areas of bare skin that come directly into contact with the eggs, permitting the direct transfer of body heat when the bird is sitting. In some birds it can be a single patch of bare skin, in others several small patches equal to the number of eggs laid. In ducks, the female bird plucks its down feathers and uses them as a nest-lining.

violet or lilac plumage

THE BIRDS YOU WILL FIND IN THIS CHAPTER

♂ Plum-coloured
Starling

♀

PURPLE GALLINULE
Wetlands. The underparts of this bird
are a deep purple-blue, appearing more
purple than blue as the bird moves.
(Grootkoningriethaan) 46 cm

PURPLE ROLLER
Woodland. This many-coloured roller
has purple shoulder-patches and
undertail coverts.
(Groottroupant) 36-40 cm

PURPLE-CRESTED LOURIE
Riverine woodland. Has a purple crest
on a shiny green head; red eye-ring
and flight feathers.
(Bloukuifloerie) 47 cm

BROAD-BILLED ROLLER
Palm savanna. This small, yellow-
billed roller has purple underparts
and cinnamon upperparts.
(Geelbektroupant) 27 cm

LILAC-BREASTED ROLLER
Bushveld. Named for its lilac breast, it
also has blue underparts and flight
feathers.
(Gewone troupant) 36 cm

SCIMITAR-BILLED WOOD HOOPOE
Woodland. Seen at close range, the head, mantle and wings are deep purple.
(Swartbekkakelaar) 24-28 cm

PLUM-COLOURED STARLING (male)
Woodland. Its iridescent upperparts appear purple or coppery; white below.
(Witborsspreeu) 18-19 cm

EUROPEAN STARLING (breeding)
Suburbia. Its green-black plumage shows a purple sheen about the upper breast and mantle.
(Europese spreeu) 20-22 cm

LONG-TAILED GLOSSY STARLING
Mopane woodland. Shows much purple in its mantle and upper tail.
(Langstertglansspreeu) 30-34 cm

purple, violet or lilac plumage

BURCHELL'S GLOSSY STARLING
Woodland. The blue plumage shows
purple in the wings, upper tail and thighs.
(Grootglansspreeu) 30-34 cm

LESSER BLUE-EARED GLOSSY STARLING
Woodland. Shows magenta thighs in good light.
(Klein-blouoorglansspreeu) 20 cm

**GREATER BLUE-EARED GLOSSY
STARLING**
Woodland. This blue-green bird shows
purple-blue flanks in good light.
(Groot-blouoorglansspreeu) 21-23 cm

YELLOW-BELLIED SUNBIRD (male)
Broad-leaved woodland. Green head and
upperparts; purple breast; yellow belly.
(Geelpenssuikerbekkie) 11 cm

BLACK SUNBIRD (male)
Woodland. Has an iridescent
purple throat and shoulder-patches.
(Swartsuikerbekkie) 15 cm

VIOLET-EARED WAXBILL
Dry thornveld. Both sexes have
violet ear coverts and red bills.
(Koningblousysie) 13-15 cm

VIOLET-BACKED SUNBIRD (male)
Broad-leaved woodland.
Chin and upperparts entirely violet; below white.
(Blousuikerbekkie) 12,5-14 cm

purple, violet or lilac plumage

birds with

including chestnut

The term rufous refers to the reddish-brown colour that is common in many birds, especially birds of prey. The colouring of the Rock Kestrel is a good example. Another brownish colour found in some bird plumages, and often mistaken for rufous, is what, for lack of a better description, is accurately called chestnut, the colour of a fruit that does not even grow in southern Africa! For the sake of those who may never have set eyes on a chestnut (even worse, not savoured the flavour of a roasted chestnut!) we include this colour in the rufous range, although it is a little more yellow than true rufous.

Spike-heeled Lark

ACCIPITERS AT REST

When perched, sparrowhawks and goshawks are notoriously difficult to approach on foot, but are often more tolerant of a motor vehicle. Since the general colouring of their upperparts is grey or dark brown according to age and sex, rather concentrate on the colours of their soft parts and the patterns of barring or streaking on their underparts. Eye colours can be yellow, deep red or dark brown; the ceres yellow, red or grey according to species and age. Yellow is by far the most common leg colour, while orange is common to some immatures and to the Ovambo Sparrowhawk. Red legs and ceres are found only in adult Gabar Goshawks. Most adult birds have close barring, rufous or grey, on their underparts, with the exception of the Gabar Goshawk which also has a grey upper breast. Immature Little Banded and Gabar Goshawks have the upper breast streaked and the belly barred, while both immature Little Sparrowhawks and African Goshawks have heavily-spotted underparts. The Rufous-breasted Sparrowhawk and some immature Ovambo Sparrowhawks stand apart in having non-barred, entirely rufous breast and belly.

rufous plumage

THE BIRDS YOU WILL FIND IN THIS CHAPTER

WHITE-BACKED NIGHT HERON
Inland rivers. Rufous neck and mantle;
black cap; yellow facial skin and legs.
(Witrugnagreier) 53 cm

DARTER (male)
Inland waters. Front of neck
rufous; crown and body very
dark brown; front of neck
sandy in female.
(Slanghalsvoël) 79 cm

GOLIATH HERON
Wetlands. Huge heron with
rufous head, neck and underparts; upperparts grey.
(Reusereier) 140 cm

RUFOUS-BELLIED HERON
Wetlands. Very dark small heron;
rich rufous below and on wings.
Bill and legs normally yellow.
(Rooipensreier) 58 cm

194 birds by colour

MACCOA DUCK (male)
Inland waters. Chestnut body; black
head with bright blue bill; stiff tail.
(Bloubekeend) 46 cm

WHITE-FACED DUCK
Wetlands. White face on black head;
rufous neck and upper breast.
(Nonnetjie-eend) 48 cm

SOUTH AFRICAN SHELDUCK
Brackish waters. Grey head (female
has white face) on rufous body;
black bill and legs.
(Kopereend) 64 cm

Br.

DABCHICK
Inland waters. Chestnut sides to
head and neck; distinctive creamy
patch at base of bill.
(Kleindobbertjie) 20 cm

EGYPTIAN GOOSE
Wetlands. Rufous neck and upper
body; pale below; pink legs.
(Kolgans) 71 cm

rufous plumage **195**

RED-CHESTED FLUFFTAIL (male)
Marshlands. Small, secretive. Head,
nape and upper breast chestnut.
(Rooiborsvleikuiken) 15-17 cm

CORNCRAKE
Rank grass. Tawny bird with chest-
nut wing coverts.
(Kwartelkoning) 37 cm

PAINTED SNIPE (female)
Pond fringes. Rufous from above the
eyes to nape and breast; olive-green
back; white on central crown, eye-stripe
and shoulders; legs yellow.
(Goudsnip) 28-32 cm

BUFF-SPOTTED FLUFFTAIL (male)
Forests. Small, secretive. Head, nape
and upper breast chestnut; buff spots
on dark back.
(Gevlekte vleikuiken) 17 cm

BAILLON'S CRAKE
Marshlands. Very small. Chestnut
above; grey below; yellowish legs.
(Kleinriethaan) 18 cm

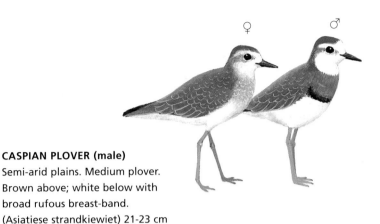

♀ ♂

CASPIAN PLOVER (male)
Semi-arid plains. Medium plover.
Brown above; white below with
broad rufous breast-band.
(Asiatiese strandkiewiet) 21-23 cm

Br.　　　　　　Non-br.

RUDDY TURNSTONE (breeding)
Shorelines. Chestnut above with black and
white about head, neck and breast; white below.
(Steenloper) 22 cm

CHESTNUT-BANDED PLOVER (male)
Salt pans. Small plover. Buff-grey above;
white below with chestnut breast-band.
(Rooibandstrandkiewiet) 15 cm

AFRICAN JACANA
Lily pans. Rufous-bodied waterbird with
long legs and toes; head and neck black
above, white below.
(Grootlangtoon) 40 cm

BURCHELL'S COURSER
Short grasslands. Mainly
chestnut colouring; grey nape;
white belly and legs.
(Bloukopdrawwertjie) 23 cm

CRESTED FRANCOLIN
Bushveld. Rufous brown above
with black and white facial marks;
well-spotted breast; red legs.
(Bospatrys) 32 cm

TEMMINCK'S COURSER
Short grasslands. Rufous cap
and lower breast; white underbelly and legs.
(Trekdrawwertjie) 23 cm

CROWNED EAGLE
Forests. Rufous underwing
coverts in flight.
(Kroonarend)
80-90 cm

HARLEQUIN QUAIL (male)
Rank grass. Chestnut underparts
with black markings (male); black-
and-white about the head.
(Bontkwartel) 18 cm

AFRICAN FISH EAGLE
Wetlands. White head,
breast and mantle on rufous
body; darker above.
(Visarend) 63-73 cm

Imm.

JACKAL BUZZARD
Mountains. Dark buzzard with rufous breast and tail; distinctive black and white underwings.
(Rooiborsjakkalsvoël) 44-53 cm

♂

♀

LITTLE BANDED GOSHAWK
Woodland. Banded rufous below chin to belly; above grey. Immature has rufous streaks and bands below.
(Gebande sperwer) 30-34 cm

RUFOUS-BREASTED SPARROWHAWK
Open woodland. Underbody and underwing coverts rufous; dark above; eyes and legs yellow.
(Rooiborssperwer) 33-40 cm

OVAMBO SPARROWHAWK (immature)
Woodland. Rufous morph of the immature has the entire head and body that colour; cere yellow; legs orange.
(Ovambosperwer) 33-40 cm

LITTLE SPARROWHAWK
Riverine forests. Entire underbody and underwings banded rufous; above grey; white spots on upper tail.
(Kleinsperwer) 23-25 cm

RED-NECKED FALCON
Kalahari thornveld. Well-barred
falcon with rufous cap and nape.
(Rooinekvalk) 36 cm

CUCKOO HAWK
Woodland. This hawk, with its crested grey
head and barred tail, is broadly-barred rufous
on breast, belly and underwing coverts.
(Koekoekvalk) 40 cm

PYGMY FALCON (female)
Dry Acacia veld. Rufous mantle; red
eye-ring, cere and legs.
(Dwergvalk) 19,5 cm

LANNER FALCON
Cliffs. Told by rufous crown; upper-
parts grey; underparts creamy-white.
(Edelvalk) 40-45 cm

TAITA FALCON
Rocky gorges. Grey above with
rufous nape-patches; rufous belly,
vent and underwing coverts.
(Taitavalk) 28 cm

HOBBY FALCON
Light woodland. Dark above;
heavily streaked below with
rufous thighs.
(Europese boomvalk) 30-35 cm

AFRICAN HOBBY FALCON
Palm woodland. Blackish head;
grey upperparts; entirely
rufous below.
(Afrikaanse boomvalk) 28-30 cm

ROCK KESTREL
Hills and grasslands. Grey head;
rufous upperwings and underparts; upper tail grey; well-barred
in female, single bar in male.
(Kransrooivalk) 30-33 cm

GREATER KESTREL
Grasslands. Entirely rufous upperparts and body; white underwings
and undertail.
(Grootrooivalk) 36 cm

LESSER KESTREL
Grasslands. Both sexes have rufous
upperwings; male has grey head,
secondary coverts, back and upper tail.
(Kleinrooivalk) 28-30 cm

rufous plumage **201**

EASTERN RED-FOOTED KESTREL (male)
Grasslands. Slate-grey above; pale grey below with rufous vent; white under-wings; red cere and legs.
(Oostelike rooipootvalk) 28-30 cm

CINNAMON DOVE
Forests. Forehead and chin white; rest rufous; wings greenish.
(Kaneelduifie) 25-30 cm

WESTERN RED-FOOTED KESTREL (male)
Grasslands. Entirely dark grey with rufous vent; dark underwings, red cere and legs.
(Westelike rooipootvalk)
28-30 cm

BURCHELL'S SANDGROUSE
Kalahari. Face grey in male; yellow in female. Below rufous; spotted white.
(Gevlekte sandpatrys) 25 cm

WESTERN RED-FOOTED KESTREL (female)
Grasslands. Head and underparts (including under-wing coverts) rufous; upperwings grey. Cere and legs red.
(Westelike rooipootvalk) 29-30 cm

ROCK PIGEON
Cliffs. Streaked neck; wings and upper body rufous; wings with white spots.
(Kransduif) 33 cm

BLACK COUCAL
Tropical marshes. Entirely black apart from rufous wings.
(Swartvleiloerie) 32-37 cm

BURCHELL'S COUCAL
Thickets. Rufous wings; black cap and tail; faint barring on upper tail coverts; underparts white.
(Gewone vleiloerie) 44 cm

SENEGAL COUCAL
Dense thickets. Rufous wings; black cap and tail; white underparts.
(Senegalvleiloerie) 41 cm

WHITE-BROWED COUCAL
Thickets. Black crown grades onto rufous mantle and wings; white eyebrow; white streaking from head to mantle.
(Witbrouvleiloerie) 44 cm

COPPERY-TAILED COUCAL
Reedbeds. Rufous wings, darker on nape; cap and tail coppery-black.
(Grootvleiloerie) 44-50 cm

PEL'S FISHING OWL
Wooded rivers. Large owl entirely chestnut-brown; dark above, paler below.
(Visuil) 63-65 cm

PURPLE ROLLER
Woodland. Large roller with rufous underparts streaked white.
(Groottroupant) 36-40 cm

GIANT KINGFISHER
Inland waters. Large black-and-white kingfisher; male with rufous breast; female with rufous belly; bill black.
(Reusevisvanger) 43-46 cm

AFRICAN HOOPOE
Woodland. Rufous crest, head and body; black and white wings.
(Hoephoep) 27 cm

GREY-HOODED KINGFISHER
Woodland. Red bill; grey head, breast and mantle; chestnut belly.
(Gryskopvisvanger) 20 cm

KAROO LARK
Karoo. Some races have rich rufous upperparts and facial colouring. (Karoolewerik) 17 cm

RED-THROATED WRYNECK
Woodland. Above speckled brown and black; below rufous throat and upper breast on creamy-white. (Draaihals) 18 cm

RUFOUS-NAPED LARK
Open bushveld. Eastern race with rufous crest and wings; body washed rufous; pale western race with rufous on wings only. (Rooineklewerik) 18-19 cm

RED LARK
Bushmanland. May have brick-red to rich rufous upperparts. (Rooilewerik) 19 cm

BARLOW'S LARK
Namib dunes. Some races have chestnut upperparts and facial colouring. (Barlowse lewerik) 19 cm

SHORT-TOED ROCK THRUSH (male)
Rocky hills. Grey above with white crown; rufous below from upper breast to vent. (Korttoonkliplyster) 18 cm

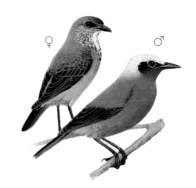

SPIKE-HEELED LARK
Grasslands and scrub. SE race has rufous colouring overall; short tail. (Vlaktelewerik) 15-16 cm

PINK-BILLED LARK
Short grasslands. SE race has rich rufous plumage; pink bill and legs. (Pienkbeklewerik) 12 cm

CHESTNUT-BACKED FINCHLARK
Grassy plains. Male has chestnut nape and wings; black head and body; white ear-patch. (Rooiruglewerik) 12-13 cm

MIOMBO ROCK THRUSH (male)
Woodland. Pale grey above to throat; upper breast rufous; belly whitish. (Angolakliplyster) 18 cm

SENTINEL ROCK THRUSH (male)
Rocky uplands. Grey head, mantle and breast; lower breast to vent rufous.
(Langtoonkliplyster) 21 cm

MOCKING CHAT (female)
Rocks with bushes. Entirely grey-black above; dark rufous below.
(Dassievoël) 20-23 cm

CAPE ROCK THRUSH
Rocky slopes and cliffs. Both sexes have rufous underparts, rump and tail; male with rufous mantle, grey head and neck; female speckled brown above.
(Kaapse kliplyster) 21 cm

STONECHAT (male)
Vleis. Mainly black upperparts; white rump and half-collar; underparts rufous.
(Gewone bontrokkie) 14 cm

CAPE ROCKJUMPER
Rocky hillsides. Male has black-and-white upperparts and throat; rufous breast and rump. Female rufous below with streaked breast; speckled above.
(Kaapseberglyster) 25 cm

WHITE-BROWED SCRUB ROBIN
Scrub. Rufous rump and upper tail coverts; well-streaked breast; white wing-markings.
(Gestreepte wipstert) 15 cm

TITBABBLER
Woodland. Greyish bird with well-streaked breast, pale eyes and rufous vent.
(Bosveldtjeriktik) 15 cm

KALAHARI ROBIN
Thornveld. Predominantly rufous above, including rump and tail coverts; whitish below.
(Kalahariwipstert) 16-17 cm

CINNAMON-BREASTED WARBLER
Dry, rocky bushveld. Dark brown above; lower breast and vent rufous.
(Kaneelborssanger) 13-14 cm

COLLARED PALM THRUSH
Palm savanna. Rufous upperparts and vent; black collar to creamy throat; grey flanks.
(Palmmôrelyster) 19 cm

ROCKRUNNER
Rocky and bushy hillsides. Heavily
streaked head and mantle; white
throat and breast; rufous back, belly
and vent.
(Rotsvoël) 17 cm

CAPE BATIS
Forest fringes. Female has rufous
throat, breast band and flanks
on white underparts; yellow
eyes; red eye-rings.
(Kaapse bosbontrokkie) 12-13 cm

RUFOUS-EARED WARBLER
Dry scrub veld. Rufous mask and
ear coverts; black breast-band on
white underparts; erect tail.
(Rooioorlangstertjie) 16 cm

CHIN-SPOT BATIS (female)
Woodland. Small rufous chin-spot
and broad rufous breast-band;
yellow eyes.
(Witliesbosbontrokkie) 12-13 cm

rufous plumage **209**

PARADISE FLYCATCHER
Woodland. Blue-black head and
breast; blue eye-rings and bill;
rufous upperparts and tail.
(Paradysvlieëvanger) 23-41 cm

BRUBRU
Woodland. Small pied bird
with rufous flanks on white
underparts.
(Bontroklaksman) 15 cm

RED-BACKED SHRIKE (male)
Bushveld. Grey head, nape and rump;
black mask; rufous mantle and back;
white underparts.
(Rooiruglaksman) 18 cm

SOUTHERN TCHAGRA
Coastal bush and thickets. Brown
crown and mantle. Rufous wings;
heavy bill.
(Grysborstjagra) 21 cm

THREE-STREAKED TCHAGRA
Thornveld thickets. Grey-brown crown
and mantle; black border to crown;
chestnut wings.
(Rooivlerktjagra) 19 cm

BLACK-CROWNED TCHAGRA
Mixed woodland. Black crown; beige
mantle; rufous wings.
(Swartkroontjagra) 21-23 cm

**SOUTHERN GREY-HEADED
SPARROW**
Chestnut upperparts with grey head;
small white wing-bar; bill black or
horn-coloured.
(Gryskopmossie) 15-16 cm

HOUSE SPARROW (male)
Human settlements. Crown grey; nape dark
brown grading into chestnut back and wings;
small white wing-bar; lores to bib black.
(Huismossie) 14 cm

CAPE SPARROW
Farmlands and suburbia. Crown, face and upper breast black in male, grey in female; mantle grey; back, rump and wings chestnut with small white wing-bar.
(Gewone mossie) 15 cm

VIOLET-EARED WAXBILL (male)
Dry thornveld. Rufous crown, wings and body; red bill and eye-rings; blue rump; black tail.
(Koningblousysie) 15 cm

GREAT SPARROW
Dry thornveld. Grey crown; chestnut nape, back and wings with small white wing-bar; male only with conspicuous black bib.
(Grootmossie) 15-16 cm

RED-BACKED MANNIKIN
Dune forests, bushveld. Black head and breast; rufous upperparts; white bill and underparts.
(Rooirugfret) 9,5-10 cm

BLACK-HEADED CANARY
Arid scrub. Both sexes have chestnut back and wings; head, throat and central breast black or black-and-white in male, greyish in female. (Swartkopkanarie) 12-15 cm

CAPE BUNTING
Various dry habitats. Black-and-white streaked head; rufous wings, crown, mantle; below washed grey-brown. (Rooivlerkstreepkoppie) 16 cm

ROCK BUNTING
Rocky koppies. Black-and-white streaked head (blackest in male); rest cinnamon-brown. (Klipstreepkoppie) 13-14 cm

rufous plumage 213

birds with dark

B rown is probably the most common plumage colour found in birds. Not only are the numerous 'little brown jobs' mostly brownish all over, but most birds of prey and many plovers, francolins and other terrestrial birds are dressed partially or entirely in brown. For those with a mainly terrestrial way of life, brown feathers or brown upperparts serve well to render the bird inconspicuous, while much the same applies to the LBJs which live in the shadowy interiors of dense thickets.

I find that many people tend to describe small brown birds as 'greyish', which is not very helpful when one is attempting to identify in retrospect the 'one that got away'. I am not sure whether this 'grey' description stems from a tendency to generalise broadly or a genuine inability to differentiate between colours. (I understand that some 40% of men have some degree of colour-blindness which, in many cases, results in their being unable to separate tones in the red-brown spectrum.) Whatever the reason, in this chapter I have selected only medium brown to dark brown birds, but I do accept that they may appear dark grey or blackish to some birders.

THE GENUS ACCIPITER

Accipiter (pronounced ak-sip-iter) is merely the Latin name for a hawk and is specifically the generic name for the sparrowhawk group of raptors – mostly small, short-winged, longish-tailed hawks. Most hunt other small birds in woodland and forest from a hidden perch, surprising their quarry in a brief, rapid and agile chase. Sparrowhawks have long, slender legs and feet with an elongated central toe. The larger species are often called goshawks, which although lacking the long central toe are basically similar.

Related to the accipiters is the genus *Melierax*, the grey chanting goshawks to which the small Gabar Goshawk rightly belongs. The two species of chanting goshawks in southern Africa are moderately large hawks with reddish ceres and long red legs (yellow in immatures). They either still-hunt for terrestrial prey from a perch or forage on the ground like small Secretarybirds.

brown colouring

THE BIRDS YOU WILL FIND IN THIS CHAPTER

REED CORMORANT (immature)
Wetlands. Entirely dark brown except for drab pale brown underbody; bill dull yellow.
(Rietduiker) 60 cm

HAMERKOP
Wetlands. Entirely dark brown waterbird; bill and legs black.
(Hamerkop) 56 cm

WHITE-BREASTED CORMORANT
Wetlands. Upperwings and tail dark brown; the wing feathers edged black.
(Witborsduiker) 90 cm

Non-br.

Br.

GLOSSY IBIS
Wetlands. Bronze-brown with iridescent green on wings; long curved bill.
(Glansibis) 71 cm

AFRICAN FINFOOT (female)
Quiet rivers. Above dark brown (grey in male); bill and legs bright red.
(Watertrapper) 63 cm

♂

♀

WOOLLY-NECKED STORK
Wooded wetlands. Dark brown above and on breast; head, neck and underbelly white.
(Wolnekooievaar) 86 cm

SPUR-WINGED GOOSE (immature)
Wetlands. Large; completely dark brown, with red bill.
(Wildemakou) 102 cm

AFRICAN BLACK DUCK
Rivers. Dark brown with white-spotted upperparts; bill grey; legs orange.
(Swarteend) 51-54 cm

SOUTHERN POCHARD
Wetlands. Female has dark upperparts only; male entirely dark brown with bronzy sheen.
(Bruineend) 51 cm

DABCHICK
Wetlands. Small waterbird; dark brown above; pale below; when breeding plumage has chestnut face and neck, and creamy spot at base of bill.
(Kleindobbertjie) 20 cm

Non-br.

Br.

MACCOA DUCK (female)
Dams with reeds. Small; dark brown with white neck and horizontal cheek-stripe; bill grey.
(Bloubekeend) 46 cm

BLACK-NECKED GREBE
Saline waters. Above dark blackish-brown; eyes red; has golden ear coverts and flanks when breeding; whitish below when not breeding.
(Swartnekdobbertjie) 28 cm

GREAT CRESTED GREBE

Wetlands. Dark brown upperparts; 'horned' crest and golden flanks when breeding; head, neck and underparts white at other times.
(Kuifkopdobbertjie) 50 cm

COMMON SANDPIPER

Inland water shorelines. Upperparts and breast-band dark brown; below white extending around the folded wing; white upper tail barred brown.
(Gewone ruiter) 20 cm

WOOD SANDPIPER

Inland water shorelines. Upperparts dark brown with white speckling; white eyebrows; buffy breast; white belly; yellow-green legs.
(Bosruiter) 20 cm

AFRICAN RAIL

Reedbeds. Dark brown above; grey below to lower breast; black-and-white barred belly and flanks; bill red.
(Grootriethaan) 36 cm

THREE-BANDED PLOVER

Inland water shorelines. Small plover told by white underparts with two black breast-bands; above dark brown; bill and eye-rings red.
(Driebandstrandkiewiet) 18 cm

BLACK-WINGED PLOVER

Grasslands. Folded upper wings dark
olive-brown; head to breast grey; large
white forehead; white belly; eyes yellow;
eye-ring red. Black-and-white underwings in flight.
(Grootswartvlerkkiewiet) 29 cm

BLACK-WINGED PRATINCOLE

Wetlands and farmlands. Dark brown
above; buff throat edged black; buff
breast; white belly and rump; underwings
show all black.
(Swartvlerksprinkaanvoël) 25 cm

ROCK PRATINCOLE

River rapids. Dark brown above,
separated from grey breast by white
collar; white belly and rump; red legs.
(Withalssprinkaanvoël) 18 cm

LESSER BLACK-WINGED PLOVER

Moist grasslands. Folded upper wings
dark olive-brown; head to breast grey;
small white forehead; eyes yellow.
Black-and-white underwings in flight.
(Kleinswartvlerkkiewiet) 23 cm

RED-WINGED PRATINCOLE

Wetlands. Dark brown above; buff throat
edged black; buff breast; white belly and
rump; underwings show red-brown.
(Rooivlerksprinkaanvoël) 25 cm

dark brown colouring **219**

CAPE FRANCOLIN
Fynbos. Large, dark francolin; dark brown above with feathers edged pale buff; black below; feathers streaked white; legs reddish.
(Kaapse fisant) 40-45 cm

NATAL FRANCOLIN
Riverine bush. Dark brown above with black streaking; speckled black and white below; bill red and yellow; legs red.
(Natalse fisant) 30-38 cm

RED-NECKED FRANCOLIN
Dense bush. Eastern races are dark brown above, streaked black; below black streaked white; all bare parts red.
(Rooikeelfisant) 32-44 cm

SWAINSON'S FRANCOLIN
Bushveld. Entirely dark brown; red facial skin and neck; dark grey legs.
(Bosveldfisant) 34-39 cm

OSTRICH (female)
Grasslands and woodland. The female has a dark brown body with some whitish wing feathers; head, neck and legs whitish.
(Volstruis) 2 m

WHITE-BACKED VULTURE (immature)
Game regions. Young birds are dark brown streaked white below; blackish head and neck with a white downy covering; no white back.
(Witrugaasvoël) 90-98 cm

J.

WHITE-HEADED VULTURE
Game regions. Dark brown back, wings and upper breast; crown, nape and below white (female has white inner secondaries); bare parts pink; bill blue and red.
(Witkopaasvoël) 85 cm

J.

CAPE GRIFFON VULTURE (immature)
Highveld and bushveld. Young birds are medium brown with pale streaks below; head, neck and breast-patches red with white downy covering.
(Kransaasvoël)105-115 cm

HOODED VULTURE
Game regions. Dark brown at all ages; adults have white legs, thighs, pectoral feathers and downy hood; neck and facial skin pink; bill slender.
(Monnikaasvoël) 70 cm

LAPPET-FACED VULTURE
Game regions. Above and wings dark brown; below white; breast streaked dark brown; head and neck red; bill horn-coloured.
(Swartaasvoël) 115 cm

YELLOW-BILLED KITE
Wide ranging. Entirely dark brown
with forked tail and yellow soft parts.
(Geelbekwou) 55 cm

BOOTED EAGLE
Dry, montane regions. Small eagle.
Above dark brown; below dark brown,
buff or white; cere and feet pale yellow.
(Dwergarend) 48-52 cm

BLACK-BREASTED SNAKE EAGLE
Bushveld. Above entirely dark brown to
head and breast; below white; underwings
with some black barring; eyes yellow.
(Swartborsslangarend) 63-68 cm

LESSER SPOTTED EAGLE
Game regions. Dark brown eagle with closely
feathered legs; immature with white spots
on folded wings. Cere and feet yellow.
(Gevlekte arend) 65 cm

BROWN SNAKE EAGLE
Woodland. Large, dark brown eagle
with yellow eyes and whitish legs.
(Bruinslangarend) 71-76 cm

WAHLBERG'S EAGLE
Woodland. Entirely blackish-brown, dark brown or white with brown wings; cere and feet yellow. In flight looks square-tailed, square-winged. (Bruinarend) 55-60 cm

LONG-CRESTED EAGLE
Hilly regions. Entirely blackish-brown with long crest; feathered legs may be dappled white; striking black-and-white underwing pattern. (Langkuifarend) 53-58 cm

STEPPE EAGLE
Game regions. Adult large, dark brown; gape and feet orange-yellow. (Steppe-arend) 75 cm

AFRICAN HAWK EAGLE
Woodland. Dark brown above; white below with dark breast-streaks; eyes, cere and feet yellow. Underwing shows white 'windows'; tail with black terminal band. (Grootjagarend) 60-65 cm

AYRES' EAGLE
Woodland. Small eagle; dark brown above; white below with light or dense dark streaking. (Kleinjagarend) 46-55 cm

dark brown colouring **223**

STEPPE BUZZARD
Open country. Plumage variable, dark brown to red-brown; darkest above; streaked and banded below. (Bruinjakkalsvoël) 45 cm

CROWNED EAGLE
Forests. Large eagle; dark brown above; heavily mottled dark below; underwings with orange-brown coverts, dark trailing edge and barred tail.
(Kroonarend) 80-90 cm

AFRICAN FISH EAGLE
Wetlands. Wings dark brown; belly chestnut-brown; head, breast and mantle white; cere and legs yellow.
(Visarend) 63-73 cm

MARTIAL EAGLE
Woodland. All dark brown except for white belly and legs with brown spots; cere grey; feet yellow.
(Breëkoparend) 78-83 cm

FOREST BUZZARD
Exotic plantations. Small buzzard; dark brown above; white below with brown blotching; central breast region usually white; flanks only blotched in immatures.
(Bosjakkalsvoël) 45 cm

AFRICAN GOSHAWK
Forests. Male grey above, female dark brown above; both barred brown below; immature browner above. Long bare legs yellow.
(Afrikaanse sperwer) 40 cm

HONEY BUZZARD
Woodland. Dark brown above with greyish head; below variable: dark brown, spotted brown on white or buff (immature); underwings well barred.
(Wespedief) 54-60 cm

JACKAL BUZZARD
Hilly regions. Dark brown all over, except for chestnut-brown breast and tail; underwings dark brown and white.
(Rooiborsjakkalsvoël) 44-53 cm

AUGUR BUZZARD
Wooded hills. Dark brown above; white below; chestnut-brown tail, white underwing edged dark.
(Witborsjakkalsvoël) 44-53 cm

AFRICAN MARSH HARRIER
Marshlands. Dark brown, long-winged hawk; paler brown below; underwings well barred; flies low.
(Afrikaanse vleivalk) 44-49 cm

BAT HAWK
Riverine forests. Entirely dark
brown hawk with pale eyes
and white legs; immature with
white breast and belly.
(Vlermuisvalk) 45 cm

DICKINSON'S KESTREL
Baobab and palm woodland.
Wings dark grey-brown; rest
grey; head and back paler; below
darker; tail well barred.
(Dickinsonse valk) 28-30 cm

OSPREY
Lakes and lagoons. Upperparts
dark brown; head with dark
mask, whitish crown; underparts
white; legs pale grey.
(Visvalk) 55-63 cm

CUCKOO HAWK
Riverine forests. Dark brown
above with crested greyish head;
throat pale grey; breast and belly
broadly barred chestnut.
(Koekoekvalk) 40 cm

TAMBOURINE DOVE
Forest fringes. Above dark
brown; eyebrow, forehead and
underparts white.
(Witborsduifie) 23 cm

MEYER'S PARROT
Woodland. Upperparts brown
except for pale blue back;
belly green; forehead and
shoulders yellow.
(Bosveldpapegaai) 23 cm

RAMERON PIGEON
Forests and plantations.
Dark, purple-brown with
grey head and purple-grey
neck; eye-rings, bill and legs
bright yellow.
(Geelbekbosduif) 40 cm

RÜPPELL'S PARROT
Dry woodland. Very dark brown
with deep-blue back and belly;
yellow shoulders.
(Bloupenspapegaai) 23 cm

BROWN-HEADED PARROT
Woodland. Brown head and
neck; body and wings green.
(Bruinkoppapegaai) 40 cm

MARSH OWL

Vleis and marshes. Dark brown above (with small 'ear' tufts); pale buff below; wings show chestnut in flight.
(Vlei-uil) 36 cm

PEARL-SPOTTED OWL

Woodland. Dark brown above well spotted white; streaked brown and white below with large white pearl-like spots.
(Witkoluil) 15-18 cm

GRASS OWL

Moist grasslands. Dark brown above with small white spots; creamy below with small brown spots; no 'ear' tufts.
(Grasuil) 34-37 cm

WOOD OWL

Forests. Dark brown above including surround of facial disc; finely barred brown on whitish underparts; no 'ear' tufts.
(Bosuil) 30-36 cm

BARRED OWL

Woodland. Dark brown above including head, with fine white barring plus band of large white wing-spots; below white with brown bars and spots.
(Gebande uil) 20 cm

SPOTTED EAGLE OWL
Widespread. Dark brown above with prominent 'ear' tufts; dark border to facial disc; below finely barred and blotched with dark brown, white and buff; eyes yellow.
(Gevlekte ooruil) 43-50 cm

PEL'S FISHING OWL
Riverine forests. Dark gingery-brown above including head; eyes dark; below pale gingery-brown with dark streaks and bars; no 'ear' tufts.
(Visuil) 65 cm

EUROPEAN SAND MARTIN
Estuaries. Small martin; above dark brown; below white with narrow brown chest-band; tail with shallow fork.
(Europese oewerswael) 12 cm

CAPE EAGLE OWL
Rocky valleys. Dark brown above with prominent 'ear' tufts; orange eyes; below buffy with brown and white blotching.
(Kaapse ooruil) 48-55 cm

BANDED MARTIN

Inland waters. Large martin; above dark brown; below white with wide brown chest-band; small white eyebrow, square tail. (Gebande oewerswael) 17 cm

PALM SWIFT

Vicinity of palm trees. Small, slender-winged brown swift with deeply forked tail. (Palmwindswael) 17 cm

BROWN-THROATED MARTIN

Inland rivers. Small martin; belly white; rest dark brown (a few birds all brown). (Afrikaanse oewerswael) 13 cm

CROWNED HORNBILL

Lowland forest fringes. Dark brown above; mostly white below; large red bill with yellow base; yellow eyes. (Gekroonde neushoringvoël) 50-57 cm

ROCK MARTIN

Cliffs. Dark brown, broad-winged; paler below; tail square with white 'windows'. (Kransswael) 15 cm

GREY HORNBILL

Mixed bushveld. Dark brown above to upper breast; wing feathers edged creamy; eyebrows white; bill black; upper mandible and casque creamy (reduced in female); below white from lower breast to vent.
(Grysneushoringvoël) 43-48 cm

WHITE-EARED BARBET

Coastal forest fringes. Dark brown with white ear-stripes and underbelly.
(Witoorhoutkapper) 18 cm

MONTEIRO'S HORNBILL

Rocky regions. Above dark brown to breast; wings with white spots; secondaries and outer tail feathers white; lower breast to vent white; bill red.
(Monteirose neushoringvoël) 54-58 cm

LESSER HONEYGUIDE

Woodland. Dark greenish-brown above; wing feathers edged paler; outer tail feathers white; breast dusky; belly white; white patch above the base of the stumpy bill.
(Kleinheuningwyser) 15 cm

BRADFIELD'S HORNBILL

Broad-leaved woodland. Bill orange with yellow base; eyes yellow; head to neck greyish; wings and tail dark brown; tail white-tipped, underparts white.
(Bradfieldse neushoringvoël) 50-57 cm

GREATER HONEYGUIDE
Woodland. Adult dark brown above with
faint yellow shoulder; male has pink bill and
dark throat-patch; female has black bill;
below whitish in both sexes; white outer tail
feathers; immature yellow below.
(Grootheuningwyser) 19-20 cm

Imm.

♀

♂

AFRICAN BROADBILL
Lowland forest fringes. Small; dark
brown above; white below streaked
brown on breast and flanks.
Makes a circular display flight in the
horizontal plane and reveals white,
puffed back feathers.
(Breëbek) 14cm

♂

♀

DUSKY LARK
Broad-leaved woodland.
Dark brown above; face and
underparts white, heavily
marked and streaked to
lower breast; legs white.
(Donkerlewerik) 19 cm

BOTHA'S LARK
Upland grasslands. Dark brown above;
all feathers with buffy fringes, throat
white; buffy below; chest well spotted;
stubby bill red.
(Vaalrivierlewerik) 12 cm

SHARP-BILLED HONEYGUIDE
Wooded regions. Small; dark brown
above with white outer tail feathers;
below white with dusky breast; bill black.
(Skerpbekheuningvoël) 13 cm

TERRESTRIAL BULBUL

Forests and thickets. Dark brown above;
white throat contrasts with dusky breast
and flanks.
(Boskrapper)
21-22 cm

RED-EYED BULBUL

Bush and gardens. Tufted head;
bill and legs black; eye-rings red;
upperparts dark brown; below
dusky white; vent yellow.
(Rooioogtiptol) 21 cm

BUSH BLACKCAP

Upland scrub on forest fringes.
Told by black cap, red bill and
legs; wings and tail dark brown;
breast grey; belly white.
(Rooibektiptol) 17 cm

CAPE BULBUL

Coastal scrub, gardens. Tufted head to
breast and upperparts dark brown;
eye-rings white; belly dusky white;
vent yellow; bill and legs black.
(Kaapse tiptol) 21 cm

BLACK-EYED BULBUL

Woodland and gardens. Tufted
head, eyes, bill and legs black;
upperparts dark brown; below
dusky white; vent yellow.
(Swartoogtiptol) 20-22 cm

dark brown colouring 233

KURRICHANE THRUSH
Broad-leaved woodland. Dark grey-brown above; eyebrows and throat white with black moustachial streaks; upper breast greyish; flanks washed orange; belly white; eye-rings, bill and legs orange.
(Rooibeklyster) 22 cm

ARROW-MARKED BABBLER
Mixed bushveld and thickets. Above dark brown; breast grey-brown; belly tawny; white arrow marks all over; eyes orange with red eye-rings; bill and legs black.
(Pylvlekkatlagter) 23-25 cm

ORANGE THRUSH
Forests. Dark brown above with two white wing-bars; throat, breast and flanks orange; belly to vent white; bill black; legs pink.
(Oranjelyster) 23 cm

HARTLAUB'S or WHITE-RUMPED BABBLER
Riverine woodland. Upperparts and breast dark brown; all feathers fringed white; rump, belly and vent white; eyes yellow with red eye-rings.
(Witkruiskatlagter) 26 cm

OLIVE THRUSH
Montane forests and gardens. Dark, olive-brown above; throat speckled black on white; under-parts orange (highveld race with brown breast); vent white or dusky; bill and legs orange-yellow.
(Olyflyster) 24 cm

SPOTTED THRUSH
Coastal forests. Above dark brown with two white wing-bars; face and under-parts white, heavily marked and spotted black; bill black; legs pink.
(Natallyster) 23 cm

SICKLE-WINGED CHAT
Grasslands and Karoo scrub. Dark brown above with rufous-edged wing feathers and pale chestnut rump; off-white below with dusky breast.
(Vlaktespekvreter) 15 cm

GROUNDSCRAPER THRUSH
Woodland. Dark grey-brown above; below white with bold black facial markings and spots; bill black above and orange below; legs pale orange.
(Gevlekte lyster) 22 cm

FAMILIAR CHAT
Rocky ground and farmyards. Dark brown above, slightly paler below, rump rich chestnut-brown, tail same with black tip and central feathers.
(Gewone spekvreter) 15 cm

MOUNTAIN CHAT (female)
Boulder-strewn slopes. Dark brown with white rump and outer tail feathers; bill and legs black.
(Bergwagter) 17-20 cm

ANT-EATING CHAT
Short grasslands. Entirely dark brown or blackish-brown; only primary feathers show paler in flight.
(Swartpiek) 18 cm

dark brown colouring **235**

BURNT-NECKED EREMOMELA
Acacia woodland. Grey-brown above; yellow-buff below; brown throat-bar not always present; pale eyes with brown eye-rings.
(Bruinkeelbossanger) 12 cm

KAROO ROBIN
Karoo. Dark brown above and only slightly paler below; white eyebrows, moustachial streaks and throat; tail-tips white; vent white spotted black.
(Slangverklikker) 17 cm

YELLOW-BELLIED EREMOMELA
Mixed bushveld or scrub. Grey-brown upperparts; pale grey breast; yellow belly; soft parts black.
(Geelpensbossanger) 9-10 cm

GARDEN WARBLER
Parks and gardens. Nondescript warbler; dark brown above; whitish below; no prominent features.
(Tuinsanger) 5 cm

BARRED WARBLER
Woodland thickets. Dark brown above, buffy below and well barred brown; has dark breast in summer.
(Gebande sanger) 13-15 cm

NEDDICKY
Thickets. Above plain dark brown except for rusty cap; below blue-grey (southern and eastern regions); buffy elsewhere. (Neddikkie) 10-11 cm

STIERLING'S BARRED WARBLER
Woodland thickets. Dark brown above; white below and well barred blackish. (Stierlingse sanger) 11,5-13 cm

RED-FACED CISTICOLA
Reedbeds and rank grass. Dark brown above; white below; face, flanks and breast washed rufous; most noticeably in winter. (Rooiwangtinktinkie) 12-13 cm

CINNAMON-BREASTED WARBLER
Upper tail black; rest of upperparts dark brown, except for cinnamon forehead; breast, flanks and rump cinnamon; throat pale with dark barring. (Kaneelborssanger) 13-14 cm

TAWNY-FLANKED PRINIA
Riverine vegetation and gardens. Dark brown above with white eye-brows and dark eye-stripe; white below; flanks, vent and rump tawny. (Bruinsylangstertjie) 10-15 cm

NAMAQUA WARBLER
Karoo scrub. Dark brown above; white below with buffy wash to flanks and vent; breast lightly spotted. (Namakwalangstertjie) 14 cm

BLACK-CHESTED PRINIA
Dry thorn scrub. Dark brown above; eyebrow to vent white with broad black breast-band; yellow below in winter. (Swartbandlangstertjie) 15 cm

KAROO PRINIA
Fynbos and Karoo scrub. Dark brown above; eyebrows and underparts very pale yellow; breast and flanks streaked black. (Karoolangstertjie) 14 cm

DUSKY FLYCATCHER
Forest fringes. Dark grey-brown above and on breast; throat and underbelly whitish; breast has indistinct dark smudges; soft parts black. (Donkervlieëvanger) 12-13 cm

SAFFRON PRINIA
Upland vleis and matted scrub. Dark brown above; eyebrows and underparts saffron-yellow; breast lightly spotted. (Gevlekte langstertjie) 14 cm

CHAT FLYCATCHER
Kalahari and Karoo. Grey-brown above; wing feather edges paler; below whitish with a brown wash to the breast and belly; soft parts black. (Grootvlieëvanger) 20 cm

SPOTTED FLYCATCHER
Woodland. Dark grey-brown above, crown streaked dark; below whitish; breast and flanks indistinctly streaked brown; soft parts black.
(Europese vlieëvanger) 14-15 cm

PALLID FLYCATCHER
Broad-leaved woodland. Dull grey-brown overall; paler on throat; soft parts black; eye-rings pale.
(Muiskleurvlieëvanger) 15-17 cm

BLUE-MANTLED FLYCATCHER
Forest fringes. Dark brown above with white wing-bar; crested head black; throat and breast black in male, finely spotted in female; belly and vent white.
(Bloukuifvlieëvanger) 17-18 cm

MARICO FLYCATCHER
Acacia thornveld. Dark brown above; clear white below; soft parts black.
(Maricovlieëvanger) 18 cm

dark brown colouring **239**

PIED STARLING

Karoo, roadsides. Very dark brown with white underbelly and vent; eyes whitish; gape orange.
(Witgatspreeu) 25-27 cm

RED-BILLED OXPECKER

Game and cattle regions. Upperparts and entire head dark brown; underparts and rump yellow-buff; bill and eyes red; eye-rings yellow.
(Rooibekrenostervoël) 20-22 cm

INDIAN MYNA

Towns. Head, mantle and breast black; rest brown; darker above; belly white; bill, facial skin and legs yellow.
(Indiese spreeu) 25 cm

RED-BILLED BUFFALO WEAVER

Mixed woodland. Red bill in both sexes; male blackish-brown, wing feather edges white, female paler on breast.
(Buffelwewer) 24 cm

YELLOW-BILLED OXPECKER

Game regions. Upperparts and entire head dark brown; underparts and rump yellow-buff; bill yellow with red tip, eyes yellow.
(Geelbekrenostervoël) 22 cm.

WHITE-BROWED SPARROW-WEAVER

Thornveld. Dark brown above with white
eyebrows, wing-bars and feather edges;
below white, with or without spotted breast;
bill black; legs pink.
(Koringvoël) 18 cm

CAPE SISKIN

Cape mountain slopes.
Dark brown above with streaky
crown; dull yellow below;
female has streaky breast.
(Kaapse pietjiekanarie) 13 cm

THICK-BILLED WEAVER

Reedbeds and adjacent bush. Male
blackish-brown all over, with a white
wing-spot and white forehead when
breeding; bill black; female dark brown
above; whitish below, heavily streaked
dark brown; bill horn-coloured.
(Dikbekwewer)18 cm

FOREST WEAVER

Forests. Dark brown above;
yellow below; throat speckled,
bill pale grey.
(Bosmusikant) 16 cm

DRAKENSBERG SISKIN

Drakensberg mountain slopes.
Dark brown above; male with
streaky head, greenish-yellow
below; female buffy below with
streaked throat and breast.
(Bergpietjiekanarie) 13 cm

birds with

including tawny-brown, buff and grey-brown

Light brown plumage, as with dark brown plumage, is mostly found on the upperparts of the bird where, on sandy terrain especially, or on mudflats, it serves to render the bird less obvious from above. On the following pages it will be seen that many birds with this colouring are shorebirds or those that frequent dry regions. In certain other species, light brown, in its various tones, is the drab plumage of female birds or males in their non-breeding plumage.

Kori Bustard

SHOREBIRDS OR WADERS
'Shorebirds' or 'waders' are two words describing the same group of birds. These are the countless small water-associated birds that migrate to southern Africa each year, arriving here in September and departing again for their northern breeding grounds in March. The term 'shorebird' accurately describes their habitat and activities; they feed in shallow water, both fresh and saline, on our coastlines and on the shores of estuaries, rivers, lagoons and most other inland waters. In the Old World the term 'wader' is commonly applied to these little greyish birds whereas in the New World 'shorebird' is used. Since the term 'wader' correctly applies also to the many large water-feeding birds such as herons, spoonbills, stilts, avocets, oystercatchers, gallinules and some plovers, the more specific American term 'shorebird' is used in this book.

light brown plumage

THE BIRDS YOU WILL FIND IN THIS CHAPTER

Tawny Eagle

DARTER (immature)
Wetlands. Young birds have pale, rufous-brown necks and bodies, becoming darker with age. (Slanghalsvoël) 79 cm

PURPLE HERON
Wetlands. Adult has red-brown neck; young birds mostly light brown; below white. (Rooireier) 89 cm

LITTLE BITTERN
Wetlands. Male has black crown, back and flight feathers (dark brown in female); rest of body, both sexes, buffy-brown, streaked white below. (Woudapie) 26 cm

♀

J.

♂

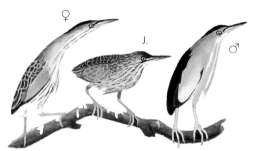

Br.

Non-br.

HADEDA IBIS
Wetlands and gardens. The head and neck are dull grey-brown; rest greenish-black with iridescent shoulder. (Hadeda) 76 cm

SQUACCO HERON
Wetlands. In breeding plumage upperparts pale red-brown; non-breeding plumage pale tawny-brown; below white. (Ralreier) 43 cm

FULVOUS DUCK
Wetlands. Head and body fulvous brown with white flank feathers; wings and back dark brown. (Fluiteend) 46 cm

CASPIAN PLOVER
Dry plains. Above light brown; sides of head and below white with dusky breast-band (non-breeding) or broad chestnut breast-band (breeding). (Asiatiese strandkiewiet) 21-23 cm

Br.   Non-br.

STRIPED CRAKE
Wetlands. Above dark brown with white feather edges; below buffy-brown. (Gestreepte riethaan) 24 cm

CHESTNUT-BANDED PLOVER
Pans and gravel pits. Light brown above; white forehead, face and underparts, with narrow chestnut or buffy throat-band. (Rooibandstrandkiewiet) 15 cm

CORNCRAKE
Rank grass. Tawny-brown all over, with black markings above and rufous wing feathers. (Kwartelkoning) 37 cm

♂

MARSH SANDPIPER
Wetlands. Above sandy-brown with white feather edges and back; below white, slender black bill; long yellow-green legs. (Moerasruiter) 23 cm

RINGED PLOVER
Wetlands. Light brown above; white below and on forehead; male has black mask and bold black band encircling breast and mantle; bill and legs orange-yellow. (Ringnekstrandkiewiet) 18 cm

KITTLITZ'S PLOVER
Wetlands. Light brown above with white and black bands around head and throat; belly white; breast buff. (Geelborsstrandkiewiet) 16 cm

GREENSHANK
Wetlands. Above sandy-brown with white feather edges and back; below white; black bill slightly upturned; long legs greenish. (Groenpootruiter) 32 cm

♀

WHITE-FRONTED PLOVER
Coastal and river shores. Sandy-brown above; male with darker forecrown; white below and on forehead. (Vaalstrandkiewiet) 18 cm

♂

LITTLE STINT
Wetlands. Small shorebird.
Non-breeding plumage sandy-brown above; feathers edged white; below white; short black bill and black legs.
(Kleinstrandloper) 14 cm

TEREK SANDPIPER
Coastal shorelines. Sandy-brown above; white below; long up-turned bill, and yellow legs.
(Terekruiter) 23-25 cm

KNOT
Shorelines. Small, bulky-bodied shorebird; sandy-brown above; white below; shortish black bill and legs.
(Knoet) 25 cm

LONG-TOED PLOVER
Floodpans. Above light brown; wing feathers white; frontal half of head and neck white; rear of head, hindneck and breast black; belly white; soft parts red.
(Witvlerkkiewiet) 30 cm

CROWNED PLOVER
Dry veld. Crown black with encircling white band; upperparts, neck and breast light brown; belly white; eyes yellow; bill and legs red.
(Kroonkiewiet) 30 cm

WATTLED PLOVER
Moist grassland. Forecrown white; rear of crown dark brown; neck streaked black; rest of upperparts and breast pale grey-brown; belly white; wattles, bill and legs yellow.
(Lelkiewiet) 35 cm

light brown plumage

WHITE-CROWNED PLOVER
Large rivers. Head grey with white central crown band; upperparts light brown; folded wings white and black; below white; wattles, bill and legs yellow.
(Witkopkiewiet)
30 cm

RÜPPELL'S KORHAAN
Desert plains. Light brown upperparts; white below; pale grey head and neck with black and white markings.
(Woestynkorhaan) 56-60 cm

BRONZE-WINGED COURSER
Woodland. Light brown above and on upper breast; dark mask; eyebrows, throat and underparts white; eye-rings and legs red.
(Bronsvlerkdrawwertjie)
25 cm

BLACK-BELLIED KORHAAN
Grasslands. Tawny above and on neck with black markings; male has black-and-white head marking plus black belly; female white below; legs pale yellow.
(Langbeenkorhaan)
58-65 cm

♀

♂

TEMMINCK'S COURSER
Short grasslands. Light brown upperparts and breast; rufous cap above white eyebrow; black eye-stripe; rufous lower breast; white belly and legs.
(Trekdrawwertjie) 20 cm

KORI BUSTARD
Woodland and grasslands. Back and wings light brown; coverts with black-and-white markings; head with crest at rear; neck grey; below white; legs pale yellow.
(Gompou) 134 cm

RED-BILLED FRANCOLIN
Dry scrub and thickets. Above light brown finely dappled black; below white with dense black barring; eye-rings yellow; bill and legs red. (Rooibekfisant) 30-38 cm

BEARDED VULTURE
Montane cliffs. Black mask and beard on white face; rest of body ginger-brown; wings and tail dark brown; eyes pale yellow and red; feet whitish. (Baardaasvoël) 110 cm

TAWNY EAGLE
Woodland. Various colour forms: light brown, tawny and gingery-brown. Tawny form only has black dappling on upperwing covert; all have black flight feathers and tail; cere and legs yellow. (Roofarend) 65-72 cm

WHITE-BACKED VULTURE
Game regions. Grey-brown above and below; back white; flight feathers, neck skin and soft parts black. (Witrugaasvoël) 90-98 cm

CAPE GRIFFON VULTURE
Wide ranging. Mature birds have wings and body feathers very pale brown; flight feathers and tail black; neck skin blue-grey; eyes honey-coloured. (Kransaasvoël) 105-115 cm

light brown plumage **249**

STEPPE EAGLE (immature)
Woodland. Immature birds light brown; can be confused with similar Tawny Eagle but for wider gape and white trailing edge to wings. (Steppe-arend) 75 cm

JACKAL BUZZARD (immature)
Hilly country. Young birds have buffy-brown bodies with dark streaks on flanks and thighs. (Rooiborsjakkalsvoël) 44-53 cm

AFRICAN HAWK EAGLE (immature)
Woodland. Young birds have entirely red-brown heads and bodies; dark brown wings; soft parts yellow. (Grootjagarend) 60-65 cm

MARTIAL EAGLE (immature)
Woodland. Young birds are light brown above; white below. (Breëkoparend) 78-83 cm

RUFOUS-BREASTED SPARROWHAWK
Wooded patches in hills. Above dark brown; below rufous-brown; underwings and tail well barred; soft parts yellow. (Rooiborssperwer) 33-40 cm

GYMNOGENE (juvenile)
Woodland. Birds in first plumage are light brown; flight feathers and tail darker; soft parts pale yellow.
(Kaalwangvalk) 60-66 cm

SPECKLED MOUSEBIRD
Bush and suburbia. Brown wings and upper tail; light brown crested head and underparts; mask and upper mandible black; lower mandible white; legs black.
(Gevlekte muisvoël) 30-35 cm

CUCKOO HAWK
Riverine woodland. Grey head; dark brown upperparts; whitish below broadly barred light brown; underwing coverts light brown.
(Koekoekvalk) 40 cm

RED-FACED MOUSEBIRD
Thornveld and suburbia. Light brown above; wings and tail darker; rump and underparts grey-white; eyes blue; bill black; mask and legs red.
(Rooiwangmuisvoël) 32-34 cm

NAMAQUA DOVE (female)
Farmlands. Light brown above with purple wing-spots; light brown breast; underparts whitish; legs maroon-red.
(Namakwaduifie) 27 cm

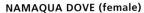

RUFOUS-NAPED LARK
Grassland with bush. Eastern birds light brown to rufous-brown, crest and wings redder; western birds paler, greyer. (Rooineklewerik) 18-19 cm

RED-CAPPED LARK
Dry pans, short grass. Light brown above with rufous cap and pectoral tufts; whitish below. (Rooikoplewerik) 15 cm

DUNE LARK
Namib dunes. Above, from head to tail, pale sanddune-brown; below white with small breast-spots. (Duinlewerik) 17 cm

BARLOW'S LARK
Scrub-vegetated dunes. Above pale red-brown from head to tail; bold facial markings; below white with boldly spotted breast. (Barlowse lewerik) 19 cm

LONG-BILLED LARK
Hills and Karoo scrublands. The paler races are light brown above; whitish below with rufous wash on spotted breast; long bill conspicuous. (Langbeklewerik) 20-22 cm

STARK'S LARK
Arid grasslands. Pale fawn above;
all feathers with dark centres;
below white, fawn wash on lightly
spotted breast; stubby bill pinkish.
(Woestynlewerik) 13 cm

KAROO CHAT
Karoo. Eastern race grey. Namibian race
has pale brown upperparts, pale brown
breast, white belly and vent; pale brown
rump and white outer tail feathers.
(Karoospekvreter) 15-18 cm

GRAY'S LARK
Desert gravel plains. Above pale fawn;
below white with fawn wash on breast;
appears all white at distance.
(Namiblewerik) 14 cm

HERERO CHAT
Arid, rocky ground. Above light brown;
rump and outer tail feathers rufous;
below white faintly streaked brown;
white eyebrow above black facial mask.
(Hererospekvreter) 17 cm

TRACTRAC CHAT
Arid plains. Southern race is light grey-
brown above; Namibian race very pale
brown, almost white above; both races
white below; rump buff or white.
(Woestynspekvreter) 14-15 cm

light brown plumage **253**

WHITE-BROWED SCRUB ROBIN
Bushveld thickets. Light brown above to below eyes; white eyebrows; rump and upper tail rufous; below white, breast and flanks streaked black. (Gestreepte wipstert) 15 cm

WHITE-CROWNED SHRIKE
Woodland. White crown; light brown mantle; dark wings; tail, lores and ear coverts, throat and breast white; belly to vent light brown. (Kremetartlaksman) 23-25 cm

GREATER DOUBLE-COLLARED SUNBIRD (female)
Upland forest fringes. Similar to Lesser Double-collared Sunbird, but bill longer than head. (Grootrooibandsuikerbekkie) 14 cm

BEARDED ROBIN
Broad-leaved and riverine woodland. Light brown above to below eyes; eyebrows white edged black; lores black; throat white; moustachial streak black; breast, flanks and rump orange; belly white. (Baardwipstert) 16-18 cm

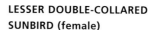

LESSER DOUBLE-COLLARED SUNBIRD (female)
Lowland woodland. Dull grey-brown overall; darker above; paler below; curved bill length of head. (Kleinrooibandsuikerbekkie) 12 cm

KALAHARI ROBIN
Kalahari thornveld. Above light brown; rump and upper tail rufous; cap grey; white eyebrows; black eye-stripe; below white washed pale rufous. (Kalahariwipstert) 16-17 cm

BLACK SUNBIRD (female)

Woodland and gardens. Light brown above; creamy-white below with creamy moustachial streak and dark mottled throat. (Swartsuikerbekkie) 15 cm

SOCIABLE WEAVER

Dry acacia woodland. Scaled light grey-brown above; cap light brown; lores and chin black; rest of underparts white. (Versamelvoël) 14 cm

MARICO SUNBIRD (female)

Thornveld. Light brown above; pale orange-yellow below with dusky throat; bill longer than head. (Maricosuikerbekkie) 13-14 cm

RED-BILLED FIREFINCH

Riverine bush. Male has upper wings grey-brown; female mostly grey-brown; lighter below; lores and rump red. (Rooibekvuurvinkie) 10 cm

LARK-LIKE BUNTING

Dry regions. Light brown above with buffy feather edges; pale eyebrows; below pale cinnamon-brown. (Vaalstreepkoppie) 14 cm

PURPLE-BANDED SUNBIRD (female)

Forest fringes. Light brown above; pale orange-yellow below with dusky throat; bill shorter than head. (Purperbandsuikerbekkie) 10-11,5 cm

birds with

including freckled, dappled, brindled and mottled

Many birds have speckled or dappled plumage as a result of individual feathers having pale margins that give a scalloped effect, or having dark centres, dark stripes or dark spots. These feathers may, in addition, be overlaid with stripes or bars of black or white, the overall result producing a confusing spotty pattern as seen, for example, in the African Snipe. In several cases these birds are best told by bill shape, bill length or colour, or leg length or colour. These features, coupled with their spotted plumage, are the surest guide to their identity.

Spotted Dikkop

WOODPECKERS

Woodpeckers are well known for their habit of tapping audibly on trees with their sharp, chisel-like beaks, but the reason for this behaviour is not always understood. The actual excavation of nest holes apart, normal tapping has the function of disturbing insects beneath the bark or loosening the bark in search of wood beetle burrows. Tapping on hollow logs is also used by many species as a means of territorial communication, a much heard woodland example of this being the far-carrying, rythmic tapping of the Bearded Woodpecker.

For actual feeding, woodpeckers are equipped with very long, sticky tongues in the case of ant and termite feeders or barbed tongues in those that feed on wood beetle grubs. In the latter, the tongue, with its backward projecting barbs, is inserted deep into the burrow of the beetle grub until the prey is hooked and extracted.

speckled plumage

THE BIRDS YOU WILL FIND IN THIS CHAPTER

*Crowned Eagle
(Immature)*

BITTERN
Wetlands. Buff above with dark crown and moustachial stripe; rest overlaid with dark brown streaks and bands; below white with dark streaks; legs whitish.
(Grootrietreier) 64 cm

WHITE-BACKED DUCK
Secluded wetlands. Head and neck buff but densely spotted black (darkest on crown); a white spot at base of black bill; rest of upperparts spotted and barred dark brown; rufous and white.
(Witrugeend) 43 cm

HOTTENTOT TEAL
Wetlands. Small duck with slate-blue bill; dark brown hood and wing feathers; mantle feathers edged white; rest of head and underparts creamy; breast to thighs spotted black.
(Gevlekte eend) 35 cm

RED-BILLED TEAL
Wetlands. Red bill; dark brown hood and upperparts; all feathers edged creamy; neck dusky; underparts white; all feathers with dark centres.
(Rooibekeend) 48 cm

CAPE SHOVELLER
Wetlands. Large drab duck. Black, broad-tipped bill; orange-yellow legs; speckled all over dark brown on pale grey; Male has paler head. In flight, shows pale blue on upper wings.
(Kaapse slopeend) 53 cm

CAPE TEAL
Brackish pans. Pale duck with pink bill. Above dark brown; feathers edged creamy; head and below white, well spotted dark brown.
(Teeleend) 46 cm

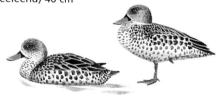

YELLOW-BILLED DUCK

Upland wetlands. Yellow bill with black saddle. Above dark brown, all feathers edged white; head and underparts white, all feathers with dark brown centres, densely so on head and neck.
(Geelbekeend) 53-58 cm

RUFF

Wetlands. Orange legs in adult, dark in immature. Head and rear of neck dappled light brown; back and wings dark brown; all feathers boldly edged white; below white.
(Kemphaan) 24-30 cm

RUDDY TURNSTONE (non-breeding)

Coastal shores. Short black bill; yellow legs. Head light brown; upperparts mottled dark brown and blackish; neck and below white; various black markings on breast plus broken black breast-band.
(Steenloper) 22 cm

AFRICAN SNIPE

Marshes. Very long, straight black bill. Head, breast and upperparts buff; heavily streaked and spotted dark brown, lower breast to belly white; flanks barred dark brown.
(Afrikaanse snip) 32 cm

GREY PLOVER (non-breeding)

Tidal flats. Bill, legs black. Above mottled light grey-brown and white; eyebrows and forehead white; below white; breast streaked light grey-brown; in flight 'armpits' black. (Grysstrandkiewiet) 30 cm

speckled plumage **259**

WHIMBREL
Coastal lagoons. Large shorebird with long, black, down-curved bill. Dark brown crown with central white stripe; above dark brown mottled white; below white, streaked brown on breast and flanks.
(Kleinwulp) 43 cm

COMMON QUAIL
Grasslands. Above rufous, mottled and streaked black and white; head with white markings; throat dark; below pale rufous; flanks streaked white.
(Afrikaanse kwartel) 18 cm

CURLEW
Tidal waters. Very large shorebird with very long, down-curved bill; head, mantle and breast buff, well streaked dark brown with buffy-white feather edges; wing feathers edged white; underbelly white.
(Grootwulp) 59 cm

GREY-WING FRANCOLIN
Grassy hills. Black bill; yellow legs. Upperparts tawny barred black and streaked white; head markings rufous; throat white well spotted black; below grey.
(Bergpatrys) 31-33 cm

SPOTTED DIKKOP
Stony grassland. Large yellow eyes; yellow bill with black tip; long yellow legs. Above buffy; heavily streaked and spotted dark brown; below white, chest streaked blackish.
(Dikkop) 44 cm

ORANGE RIVER FRANCOLIN
Dry grasslands. Legs dull yellow. Above dark grey-brown, mottled black with white streaks; head rufous, black and white; throat white; below rufous (paler in west) spotted and dappled red-brown.
(Kalaharipatrys) 33-35 cm

SHELLEY'S FRANCOLIN

Grassy woodland. Legs dull yellow.
Above dark grey-brown, blotched black
and streaked white; throat white;
below white, breast blotched red-
brown, belly barred black.
(Laeveldpatrys) 33 cm

RED-WING FRANCOLIN

Grassy hills. Legs dull yellow. Above dark
brown, blotched black and streaked white;
ear coverts and lateral neck rufous; throat
white; upper breast mottled black and
white; underparts pale rufous streaked
red-brown.
(Rooivlerkpatrys) 38-40 cm

NATAL FRANCOLIN

Granite koppies. Bill yellow and red;
legs red. Above dark brown streaked
black; below throat to vent speckled
black and white.
(Natalse fisant) 30-38 cm

BEARDED VULTURE (immature)

Maluti mountains. Bill and legs whitish;
eyes yellow; head, beard and upper breast
dark brown; rest of plumage (except flight
feathers) dappled dark and light brown
and white.
(Baardaasvoël) 110 cm

CROWNED EAGLE (immature)

Forests. Eyes and feet orange-yellow.
Above dark brown, all feathers edged
white; head and underparts white, dappled and barred dark brown and orange.
(Kroonarend) 80-90 cm

DOUBLE-BANDED SANDGROUSE (female)

Broad-leaved woodland. Normally accompanied by male. Above and breast pale yellow-buff, finely barred black; white spot on back; below finely barred black. (Dubbelbandsandpatrys) 25 cm

YELLOW-THROATED SANDGROUSE (female)

Kalahari. Face and throat yellow; crown, hindneck, upperparts and breast pale yellow heavily dappled blackish; belly dusky; vent rufous. (Geelkeelsandpatrys) 30 cm

BURCHELL'S SANDGROUSE (female)

Sandveld. Yellow face and throat. Above olive-brown spotted white; breast rufous spotted white; belly white barred rufous. (Gevlekte sandpatrys) 25 cm

NIGHTJARS

These birds are all heavily mottled, barred and spotted rufous, dark brown, black and white. Can only be specifically identified by call or by wing and tail patterns. (Naguile) 23-28 cm

 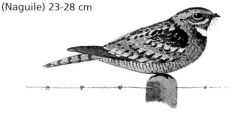

NAMAQUA SANDGROUSE (female)

Desert. Head ochre; crown rufous; upperparts whitish heavily barred dark brown and black; below yellowish, streaked and barred black; underbelly not barred. (Kelkiewyn) 28 cm

SPOTTED CREEPER

Broad-leaved woodland. Slender, down-curved bill. Upperparts dark brown heavily spotted white; underparts white, finely scalloped brown. (Boomkruiper) 15 cm

CHESTNUT-BACKED FINCHLARK (female)

Bare areas in grassland. Bill white; legs grey. Crown, nape and upperparts dappled dusky and black; hindcollar white; carpal region chestnut; wing feathers edged white; breast white dappled black; belly black.
(Rooiruglewerik) 12 cm

BLACK CUCKOOSHRIKE (female)

Woodland. Gape orange. Above dull olive-brown; wings and tail black; all feathers edged yellow; below white heavily barred black.
(Swartkatakoeroe) 22 cm

BLACK-EARED FINCHLARK (female)

Scrublands. Bill and legs white. Upperparts dappled dusky; ear coverts rufous; wings rufous dappled black, pale feather edges; below white streaked black.
(Swartoorlewerik) 12-13 cm

EUROPEAN STARLING (non-breeding)

Suburbs. Bill black; legs dark red. Above light brown heavily spotted tawny; wing feathers edged tawny; below greenish-black spotted white.
(Europese spreeu) 20-22 cm

GREY-BACKED FINCHLARK (female)

Scrublands and desert. Bill and legs white. Crown dusky; upperparts greyish; all feathers broadly edged white; breast streaked black; belly black.
(Grysruglewerik) 12-13 cm

CUT-THROAT FINCH (female)

Dry woodland. Bill and legs white. Head and breast white but well barred black, above rufous barred black, feather edges paler, below white, washed rufous.
(Bandkeelvink) 12 cm

speckled plumage 263

birds with collars

C ollars or bands are found in many bird species and are excellent recognition features. Collars, as the term suggests, refer to bands of colour that span the bird's neck or throat. In most cases the collar is to the front of the neck, but in some it spans the hindneck only, as in Kittlitz's Plover. In others, for example the Ringed Plover, it completely encircles the bird's lower neck.

The term 'breast-band' is applied to bands of colour, often black, that span the bird's breast or chest. Breast-bands may number as many as three, as in the Three-banded Plover, although a single band is most common. Some birds have a wide breast-band, for example the Bokmakierie, and these are usually called 'gorgets'.

In a few species the breast-band is found only in the male bird during the breeding season and fades or disappears completely during the non-breeding season, an example being the Black-chested Prinia.

BROOD PARASITES

These are birds that lay their eggs in the nest of an unrelated species and take no part in raising their own young. While cuckoos are well known for this behaviour, within our region there are other species that practice brood parasitism. These are the honeyguides, the whydahs and related widow finches, and the Cuckoo Finch. Most of our cuckoos are summer visitors that parasitise a range of other species according to their preferences. The common Red-chested Cuckoo favours the robin group, while the equally common Diederik Cuckoo prefers weavers and bishops. In both of these species the cuckoo egg normally hatches before those of the host, and the chick ejects the eggs of its foster siblings. Young honeyguides also hatch early and are initially equipped with a sharp bill-hook which is used to break the eggs of its host or to kill the chicks. In contrast, the whydahs and widow-finches parasitise mostly waxbills and other small finches. The parasite's chicks resemble those of the host in several ways, and grow up in harmony with them. The Cuckoo Finch, a parasitic weaver, usually parasitises cisticolas and prinias and, as far as is known, the chick does not deliberately dispose of its foster siblings.

and breast-bands

THE BIRDS YOU WILL FIND IN THIS CHAPTER

Three-banded plover

PAINTED SNIPE
Swamps. In both sexes the white underparts extend as a white band, bordered black, over the bird's mantle.
(Goudsnip) 28-32 cm

RINGED PLOVER
Inland shorelines. The black gorget extends as a narrow hindcollar parallel with the extension of the white throat.
(Ringnekstrandkiewiet) 18 cm

CASPIAN PLOVER
Dry plains. The male in breeding plumage has a wide rufous gorget, bordered black below; throat and below white.
(Asiatiese strandkiewiet) 21-23 cm

THREE-BANDED PLOVER
Inland shorelines. Two black and one white band on upper breast, the upper black and white bands encircling the neck.
(Driebandstrandkiewiet) 18 cm

CHESTNUT-BANDED PLOVER
Coastal sandflats. The chestnut collar of the male is paler in the female, grey in the immature; underparts white.
(Rooibandstrandkiewiet) 15 cm

KITTLITZ'S PLOVER
Inland shorelines. The black mask and ear coverts extend as a black hindcollar parallel with the extension of its white eyebrows.
(Geelborsstrandkiewiet) 16 cm

RUDDY TURNSTONE
Coastal shorelines. In breeding plumage the black facial and mantle markings extend as a breast-band; less distinct in non-breeding plumage.
(Steenloper) 22 cm

BRONZE-WINGED COURSER
Broad-leaved woodland. The light brown throat is separated from the white underparts by a narrow black breast-band.
(Bronsvlerkdrawwertjie) 25 cm

LONG-TOED PLOVER
Floodplains. The black nape extends to the breast to form a very wide breast-patch or gorget.
(Witvlerkkiewiet) 30 cm

CROWNED PLOVER
Dry grasslands. The light brown upperparts and breast terminate in a black band across the lower breast; a white head-band encircles the black cap.
(Kroonkiewiet) 30 cm

DOUBLE-BANDED COURSER
Dry grasslands. Two narrow black breast-bands on white underparts.
(Dubbelbanddrawwertjie) 22 cm

THREE-BANDED COURSER
Dry woodland. The white throat has a chestnut V-shaped collar; the upper breast has a dark brown breast-band extending to the shoulders, and a chestnut lower breast-band.
(Driebanddrawwertjie) 28 cm

KORI BUSTARD

Dry woodland and grasslands. The greyish neck of this huge bird is separated from its upper breast by a broken black band.
(Gompou) 135 cm

DOUBLE-BANDED SANDGROUSE

Broad-leaved woodland. The male has black and white bands on its forehead and breast.
(Dubbelbandsandpatrys) 25 cm

AFRICAN MARSH HARRIER (immature)

Marshes. Young birds are dark brown with a diagnostic broad white breast-band.
(Afrikaanse vleivalk) 44-49 cm

NAMAQUA SANDGROUSE

Desert. The male's lower breast has a white breast-band bordered below by a rufous one.
(Kelkiewyn) 28 cm

OSPREY

Lagoons and inland waters. Adults have white underparts with a broad, broken, light brown breast-band.
(Visvalk) 55-63 cm

YELLOW-THROATED SANDGROUSE

Kalahari. The male's yellow throat is bordered by a black collar.
(Geelkeelsandpatrys) 30 cm

AFRICAN MOURNING DOVE
Riverine woodland. A grey-headed, yellow-eyed dove with a black hindcollar. (Rooioogtortelduif) 30 cm

RED-CHESTED CUCKOO
Woodland. A grey cuckoo with a broad, dull orange band on the upper breast. (Piet-my-vrou) 28 cm

RED-EYED DOVE
Woodland. A large, pink-breasted dove with red eyes and a broad hindcollar. (Grootringduif) 33-36 cm

WHITE-THROATED SWALLOW
Wetlands. Clear white underparts with a black breast-band. (Witkeelswael) 17 cm

EUROPEAN SWALLOW
Widespread. Dull orange chin bordered below by a broad black collar. (Europese swael) 18 cm

CAPE TURTLE DOVE
Widespread. A grey dove with black eyes and a black hindcollar. (Gewone tortelduif) 28 cm

SWALLOW-TAILED BEE-EATER
Dry woodland. Yellow chin and throat
bordered below by a broad blue collar.
(Swaelstertbyvreter)
20-22 cm

(EUROPEAN) SAND MARTIN
Estuaries. Small. Brown above; white
below with a narrow brown breast-band.
(Europese oewerswael) 12 cm

BANDED MARTIN
Inland waters. Large. Dark brown above;
white below with a broad, dark brown
breast-band.
(Gebande oewerswael) 17 cm

LITTLE BEE-EATER
Riverine bush. Yellow throat
separated from rufous
underparts by a V-shaped
black band on upper breast.
(Kleinbyvreter) 17 cm

ALPINE SWIFT
Mountains. Large, dark brown
swift with white underparts; dark
brown breast-band and vent.
(Witpenswindswael) 22 cm

EUROPEAN BEE-EATER
Widespread. Blue forehead and underparts; yellow throat bordered below by
a small black collar.
(Europese byvreter) 25-29 cm

PIED KINGFISHER
Wetlands. Male has a double black breast-band, the upper one broad, the lower one narrow. Female has a single broad breast-band with a gap in the centre.
(Bontvisvanger) 28-29 cm

PINK-THROATED LONGCLAW
Marshlands. The red throat is bordered below by a black collar.
(Rooikeelkalkoentjie) 20 cm

YELLOW-THROATED LONGCLAW
Grasslands. Yellow below, chin to vent, with a black gorget extending from the gape.
(Geelkeelkalkoentjie) 20 cm

ORANGE-THROATED LONGCLAW
Grasslands. The orange throat is separated from the yellow underparts by a black border ending in a V shape on the lower neck.
(Oranjekeelkalkoentjie) 20 cm

LONG-TAILED WAGTAIL
Mountain streams. Very long tail; below white with a narrow black breast-band.
(Bergkwikkie) 19-20 cm

collars and breast-bands **271**

CAPE WAGTAIL

Wetlands and gardens. Greyish wagtail with white throat and upper breast; black breast-band.
(Gewone kwikkie) 18 cm

CAPPED WHEATEAR

Burnt fields and short grass. Broad black gorget extending from the ear coverts. Throat and lower breast white.
(Hoëveldskaapwagter) 18 cm

AFRICAN PIED WAGTAIL

Lowland rivers. Above black and white; below white with a broad black breast-band.
(Bontkwikkie) 20 cm

BAR-THROATED APALIS

Forests and woodland. Grey above; white or yellow below; all races have a black collar.
(Bandkeelkleinjantjie) 12-13 cm

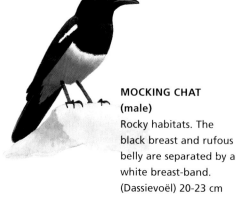

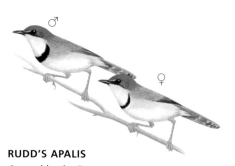

MOCKING CHAT
(male)
Rocky habitats. The black breast and rufous belly are separated by a white breast-band.
(Dassievoël) 20-23 cm

RUDD'S APALIS

Coastal bush. Grey cap; green upperparts; white below with black collar.
(Ruddse kleinjantjie) 10-12 cm

YELLOW-BREASTED APALIS
Bushveld. Below white with yellow breast; lower breast may have a small black breast-bar, often absent. (Geelborskleinjantjie) 10-12 cm

RUFOUS-EARED WARBLER
Karoo scrub. Rufous facial patch; white below with a black breast-band. (Rooioorlangstertjie) 14 cm

BURNT-NECKED EREMOMELA
Woodland. Grey above; creamy below with a small brown throat-bar, often absent. (Bruinkeelbossanger) 12 cm

PRIRIT BATIS
Dry thornveld. The male is grey above and white below, with a broad black breast-band. (Priritbosbontrokkie) 12 cm

BLACK-CHESTED PRINIA
Dry thornveld. White below when breeding, with a black breast-band; underparts yellow in non-breeding plumage. (Swartbandlangstertjie) 13-15 cm

CAPE BATIS
Forest fringes. Male has a broad black breast-band and rufous flanks. Female has rufous throat, flanks and breast-band. (Kaapse bosbontrokkie) 12-13 cm

CHIN-SPOT BATIS
Woodland. Male is white below with a
broad black breast-band. Female is white
below with a rufous chin-spot and broad
rufous breast-band.
(Witliesbosbontrokkie) 12-13 cm

BOKMAKIERIE
Bush and suburbia. Grey
cap and mantle; olive-
green wings; below yel-
low with a black gorget.
(Bokmakierie) 23 cm

WATTLE-EYED FLYCATCHER
Riverine and coastal thickets. Male has a
narrow black breast-band on white underparts. Female has a black breast.
(Beloogbosbontrokkie) 18 cm

LESSER DOUBLE-COLLARED SUNBIRD
(male)
Lowland bush. Glossy-green above,
extending around neck; blue and narrow
red breast-band; belly greyish.
(Kleinrooibandsuikerbekkie) 12,5 cm

GORGEOUS BUSH SHRIKE
Bushveld and forest fringes. Scarlet throat,
black gorget and yellow underparts.
(Konkoit) 20 cm

GREATER DOUBLE-COLLARED SUNBIRD (male)

Montane bush. Glossy-green above, extending around neck; blue and broad red breast-band.
(Grootrooibandsuikerbekkie) 14 cm

RED-COLLARED WIDOW (male)

Grassy bushveld. When breeding, the all-black, long-tailed male has a red collar. (Rooikeelflap) 40 cm

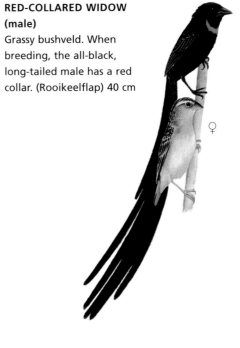

MARICO SUNBIRD

Bushveld. Glossy-green above, extending around neck; lower breast has purple and ruby-red breast band; belly black.
(Maricosuikerbekkie) 13-14 cm

CUT-THROAT FINCH (male)

Broad-leaved woodland. The white-billed, scaly-looking male has a broad red collar.
(Bandkeelvink) 12 cm

ORANGE-BREASTED SUNBIRD (male)

Fynbos. Head, mantle and throat green; upper breast has purple breast-band; underparts orange.
(Oranjeborssuikerbekkie) 15 cm

birds with crests

C rests are extended feathers, stiff or floppy, on the crowns of some birds. They may be more or less permanent tufts, as in some bulbuls and flycatchers, while in others, such as the African Hoopoe, they can be erect or lowered. In several birds the crest is only raised in alarm or in display. A good example of its use in display can be seen in the Red-crested Korhaan, which erects its crest only in courtship.

The Crowned Eagle has a lateral crest formed by raising its rear crown feathers in agitation or in conflict situations, giving the eagle a formidable appearance.

Head-plumes are mostly long and floppy and extend from the rear of the crown, as in the Secretarybird and the Kori Bustard, but in a few cases they are short and fairly stiff, as in the Crowned Crane.

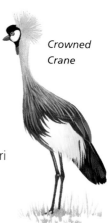

Crowned Crane

KESTRELS

Kestrels are a group of small falcons. They share certain characteristics of their larger cousins in that they have pointed wings and build no nest of their own. However, they feed on small rodents, reptiles and small birds caught mostly on the ground, or on flying insects caught on the wing. The summer-visiting Lesser and Red-footed kestrels are gregarious and hunt in flocks over grasslands, catching especially grasshoppers and flying termites. The resident kestrels mostly hunt from a roadside post or wire, making short aerial forays to catch their prey on the ground before returning with it to feed on their perch. The flight of the kestrel is graceful, with much hovering. The kestrels and the falcons have greatly increased their feeding and breeding ranges in southern Africa through man's provision of roadside perches, especially Eskom's pylons (towers) where crows and other birds of prey build their nests, which in turn, are used by the falcons and kestrels.

and head-plumes

THE BIRDS YOU WILL FIND IN THIS CHAPTER

African Hoopoe

BANK CORMORANT

Coastal. Large black cormorant with a small permanent crest just forward of its yellow eyes.
(Bankduiker) 75 cm

SQUACCO HERON

Inland waters. Breeding plumage has dark plumes extending from the rear-crown, which rest on the nape.
(Ralreier) 43 cm

CROWNED CORMORANT

Coastal. Small black cormorant with permanent crest; yellow eyes and lower mandible.
(Kuifkopduiker) 54 cm

BLACK EGRET

Inland waters. Long grey plumes hanging freely from the rear-crown; feet yellow.
(Swartreier) 66 cm

REED CORMORANT

Inland and coastal waters. Male has a small crest on its forehead; bill yellow; eyes red.
(Rietduiker) 60 cm

SLATY EGRET

Inland waters. Slate-grey with long plumes hanging freely from the rear-crown; throat rufous; legs and feet yellow.
(Rooikeelreier) 60 cm

BLACK-CROWNED NIGHT HERON

Inland waters. Black crown and back with two long, white plumes extending from the rear-crown; white below; wings grey.
(Gewone nagreier) 64 cm

PURPLE HERON

Inland waters. Grey above with rufous neck; black cap extending to two plumes from the rear-crown.
(Rooireier) 89 cm

LITTLE EGRET

Inland waters. Entirely white with long, free-hanging plum extending from the rear-crov feet yellow.
(Kleinwitreier) 64 cm

BLACK-HEADED HERON

Grasslands. Grey heron with black hood and rear-neck; two plumes extending from rear-crown.
(Swartkopreier) 97 cm

GREY HERON

Inland waters. Grey above; white head and neck; black brow extending as two plumes from the rear-crown.
(Bloureier) 100 cm

GREAT CRESTED GREBE

Inland waters. In breeding
plumage the black crown extends
backward as two pointed crests
that can be fanned.
(Kuifkopdobbertjie) 50 cm

CROWNED CRANE

Reedbeds and estuaries. Mostly grey bird
with black crown and a stiff, permanent
fan-shaped golden crest.
(Mahem) 105 cm

RED-CRESTED KORHAAN

Woodland. Rufous crest not normally
visible, erect from nape in courtship;
above brown with creamy arrow shapes.
(Boskorhaan) 53 cm

CRESTED FRANCOLIN

Bushveld. Rufous above; dark
crown feathers raised in alarm;
tail is held raised.
(Bospatrys) 32 cm

KORI BUSTARD

Woodland and grasslands.
Huge bird with blackish plumes
extending from rear-crown.
(Gompou) 135 cm

CRESTED GUINEAFOWL

Riverine forests. Neck and crown black; crown feathers elongated to form a floppy crest; bill white; body black with small blue spots. (Kuifkoptarentaal) 50 cm

Imm.

CROWNED EAGLE

Forests. When excited the entire rear-crown is raised; eyes yellow; gape and feet orange. (Kroonarend) 80-90 cm

SECRETARYBIRD

Grasslands. Large grey and black bird with long, black and grey nape feathers; facial skin orange. (Sekretarisvoël) 125-150 cm

MARTIAL EAGLE

Woodland. Does not normally appear crested but loose rear-crown feathers tend to form a crest when lifted by wind. (Breëkoparend) 78-83 cm

LONG-CRESTED EAGLE

Wooded valleys. Dark brown eagle with long, upstanding crest; unmistakable. Eyes and gape pale yellow. (Langkuifarend) 53-58 cm

KNYSNA LOURIE
Forests. The green, white-edged crest is a permanent feature, and is longer in northern races.
(Knysnaloerie) 47 cm

OSPREY
Lagoons and large dams. Loose rear-crown feathers can be raised; head and below white; yellow eyes on dark mask.
(Visvalk) 55-63 cm

GYMNOGENE
Wooded habitats. At all ages the nape feathers are raised to form a ruff when excited.
(Kaalwangvalk) 60-66 cm

CUCKOO HAWK
Riverine forests. Small, back-ward-projecting crest at the rear-crown at all ages.
(Koekoekvalk) 40 cm

PURPLE-CRESTED LOURIE
Riverine woodland. Purple-blue crest is a permanent feature; green head; eye-ring red; bill black.
(Bloukuifloerie) 47 cm

SPECKLED MOUSEBIRD
Bush and suburbia. Permanent loose
crest on head; over all brownish;
bill black above; white below.
(Gevlekte muisvoël) 30-35 cm

STRIPED CUCKOO
Woodland. Black above; head
with backward-projecting crest;
below white; throat and breast
spotted black.
(Gestreepte nuwejaarsvoël) 38-40 cm

WHITE-BACKED MOUSEBIRD
Dry bush and suburbia. Grey above
with upstanding crest; back white;
bill white with black tip.
(Witkruismuisvoël) 30-34 cm

JACOBIN CUCKOO
Woodland. Both colour morphs have
a crest projecting backward from the
black head; white morph unspotted.
(Bontnuwejaarsvoël) 33-34 cm

GREAT SPOTTED CUCKOO
Savanna. Adult has backward-
projecting crest on its grey head;
upperparts black spotted white;
below white.
(Gevlekte koekoek) 38-40 cm

RED-FACED MOUSEBIRD
Moist woodland and suburbia.
Light brown above with
backward-projecting crest;
mask red; eyes blue.
(Rooiwangmuisvoël) 32-34 cm

crests and head-plumes 283

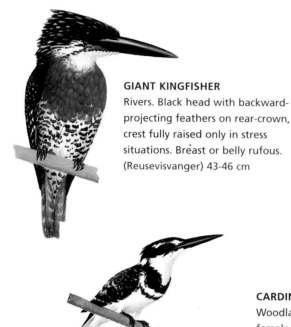

GIANT KINGFISHER
Rivers. Black head with backward-projecting feathers on rear-crown, crest fully raised only in stress situations. Breast or belly rufous. (Reusevisvanger) 43-46 cm

CRESTED BARBET
Woodland and suburbia. Yellow, red-speckled head with black, backward-projecting crest; bill cream. (Kuifkophoutkapper) 23 cm

PIED KINGFISHER
Inland waters. Black-and-white kingfisher; black crown with backward-projecting crest. (Bontvisvanger) 28-29 cm

CARDINAL WOODPECKER
Woodland. Male with red crown, female with black crown, frequently raised as a crest while feeding. (Kardinaalspeg) 14-16 cm

AFRICAN HOOPOE
Woodland. Large, rufous crest is normally held flat, but is raised when landing or when alarmed. (Hoephoep) 27 cm

RUFOUS-NAPED LARK
Grassland with bushes. Rufous crown raised; wings fluttered frequently while singing. (Rooineklewerik) 18-19 cm

STARK'S LARK
Arid grasslands. A small, pale lark with a crested head imparting a 'peaked' appearance.
(Woestynlewerik) 13 cm

BLUE-MANTLED FLYCATCHER
Forest edges. Male blue-black above, female brown; both with crested heads, longest in male; below white.
(Bloukuifvlieëvanger) 17-18 cm

♂

BLACK-EYED BULBUL
Suburbia. The black head is permanently crested; eyes black.
(Swartoogtiptol) 20-22 cm

♀

PARADISE FLYCATCHER
Woodland. Blue-grey, permanently crested head in both sexes; blue eye-rings and bill; rufous upperparts.
(Paradysvlieëvanger) 23-41 cm

RED-EYED BULBUL
Bush and suburbia. Black head permanently crested; eye-ring red.
(Rooioogtiptol) 19-21 cm

WHITE HELMET SHRIKE
Bushveld. Grey crown has stiff forehead feathers that project forward; eyes and eye-rings yellow.
(Withelmlaksman) 20 cm

crests and head-plumes **285**

flight patterns

of some larger birds, mainly from below

Eastern White Pelican

Small birds are not easy to recognise in flight simply, because of their size and rapid movements, but the larger, slower flying birds often soar with their wings firmly outstretched and present good opportunities for study. The larger herons, for example, invariably fly at low altitudes and flap their wings slowly so that, with the aid of binoculars, their details can be seen. Remember that herons, unlike storks and cranes, fly with their necks tucked-in. Remember also that the two most common large herons are easily identified in flight. The Grey Heron has entirely grey underwings, while the similar Black-headed Heron has two-tone black and grey underwings. Herons seldom soar, but storks often do, their necks and legs extended.

The larger birds of prey spend much of the day soaring, circling around in rising warm air. Their flight action is moderately slow and usually affords ample time for their wing shape and underwing pattern to be seen. With practise, the technique of focusing binoculars on flying birds will become second nature.

ACCIPITERS IN FLIGHT

The underwings and undertails of most sparrowhawks and goshawks are surprisingly similar, the common arrangement being a confusion of greyish transverse bars on the underwings and four dark bars on the undertail. The entire pattern, together with the barred underbody, is of little help in species identification during the brief glimpse normally presented to an observer by these fast-flying little hawks. In the field it is better to concentrate on seeing the bird's rump and upper tail which is usually possible as the bird banks and turns. Individual rump or tail patterns are the key to certain identification. The Little Sparrowhawk has a white bar on the rump plus two distinctive white spots on the central tail; the Little Banded Goshawk has entirely grey upperparts; the Gabar Goshawk has a bold white rump patch (absent only in the melanistic form); and the Ovambo Sparrowhawk shows white tail feather-shafts when a good view is obtained.

THE BIRDS YOU WILL FIND IN THIS CHAPTER

UNDERWINGS AND BODIES THAT ARE MOSTLY WHITE

CATTLE EGRET
Look for yellow bill and
legs; in summer look for
rufous breast. Flies with
head tucked in.
(Veereier)

GREY HERON
Yellow bill and legs; grey
underwings; slow wing beats.
Head tucked in.
(Bloureier)

SPOONBILL
Spatulate red bill; neck
extended; long red legs
trailing.
(Lepelaar)

LITTLE EGRET
Look for black bill and legs;
yellow feet. Head tucked in.
(Kleinwitreier)

SACRED IBIS
Black head and neck extended;
black legs; black trailing edge
to wings; red 'armpits'.
(Skoorsteenveër)

GREAT WHITE HERON
Yellow bill; black legs trailing;
head tucked in; slow wing beats.
(Grootwitreier)

BLACK-SHOULDERED KITE
Black tips to white underwings;
often hovers for long periods,
glides or flaps fast.
(Blouvalk)

BLACK-BREASTED SNAKE EAGLE
Dark brown head and breast; fine brown
barring on underwings and tail. Seldom
flaps, frequently hovers.
(Swartborsslangarend)

PALLID HARRIER
Narrow black tips to long wings;
above pale grey; flies low with
slow wing beats.
(Witborsvleivalk)

AUGUR BUZZARD
Black edges to wings; female has black
head; rufous tail; seldom flaps.
(Witborsjakkalsvoël)

BLACK-AND-WHITE UNDERWINGS OR BODIES

EASTERN WHITE PELICAN
Black flight feathers; large yellowish
bill; neck tucked in; slow wing
beats, often soars.
(Witpelikaan)

CAPE GANNET
Flight feathers and tail black.
Flies over the sea and plunges
for fish. Crown and nape yellow.
(Witmalgas)

SADDLE-BILLED STORK
White below except for black underwing coverts; black head and neck extended; legs trailing; large red and black bill; wing beats slow.
(Saalbekooievaar)

ABDIM'S STORK
Underwings and tail black; body white extending onto wings; head and neck black, outstretched; bill horn-coloured; trailing legs white; flocks soar. Summer.
(Kleinswartooievaar)

MARABOU STORK
Underwings and tail black; body and 'armpits' white; neck tucked in; large bill horn-coloured; trailing legs whitish. Wing beats slow, may soar.
(Maraboe)

WHITE STORK
Black flight feathers; neck stretched out; bill and trailing legs red; flocks soar. Summer.
(Witooievaar)

YELLOW-BILLED STORK
Flight feathers black; rest of underwings pinkish with narrow, parallel red bars; white head and neck outstretched; trailing legs red. Wing beats slow, soars often.
(Nimmersat)

BLACK STORK
Underwings and tail black; body white; black head and neck stretched out; bill and trailing legs red. Wing beats slow.
(Grootswartooievaar)

GREATER FLAMINGO
Slender white neck stretched out; red legs trailing; wings red and black. Fast-flapping.
(Grootflamink)

PALM-NUT VULTURE
Body white; underwings and rounded tail black and white. Flaps slowly, may soar. (Witaasvoël)

KNOB-BILLED DUCK
Black underwings and tail; bulky, white body with dusky neck and head outstretched; legs do not extend. (Knobbeleend)

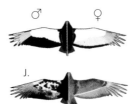

BATELEUR
Body black; short tail rufous; underwings white with broad black trailing edge in the male, narrow in the female. Flies fairly low, rocks side to side. (Berghaan)

WATTLED CRANE
Black body and flight feathers; grey underwings; white head and neck stretched out; black legs extend beyond tail. Flight ponderous. (Lelkraanvoël)

WHITE-HEADED VULTURE
White body with black breast; underwings black with white inner secondaries in the female; tail black; head tucked in. Soars. (Witkopaasvoël)

EGYPTIAN VULTURE
Body and diamond-shaped tail white; underwings black and white. Flaps slowly. (Egiptiese aasvoël)

BROWN SNAKE EAGLE
Body and underwing coverts dark brown; rest of wings whitish; tail well barred dark brown and white. (Bruinslangarend)

Imm.

LONG-CRESTED EAGLE
Body and underwing coverts black; secondaries dusky; conspicuous white 'windows' in outer wings; tail banded black and white. (Langkuifarend)

J.

MARTIAL EAGLE
Body white with black breast; underwings dark. In immature, body and underwing coverts white, only tail and flight feathers dark. Soars. (Breëkoparend)

BLACK EAGLE
Entirely black below except for white 'windows' at the base of primaries. (Witkruisarend)

Imm.

J.

Imm.

BLACK HARRIER
Body and underwing coverts black; rest of wing white with thin black trailing edge; tail banded black and white. Flies low, may hover briefly. (Witkruisvleiarend)

JACKAL BUZZARD
Underwing coverts black; tips of primaries and trailing edge of wing black; rest of wing white; tail rufous; body black and rufous. Soars. (Rooiborsjakkalsvoël)

BLACK-AND-GREY UNDERWINGS AND BODIES

GREY HERON
Yellow bill and legs; grey underwings; slow wing beats. Head tucked in. (Bloureier)

BLACK-HEADED HERON
Body and underwings grey, except for black flight feathers. (Grey Heron underwings have no black.) Neck tucked in. Wing beats slow. (Swartkopreier)

BLUE CRANE
Entirely grey except for black flight feathers. Flies with neck outstretched and legs trailing. Wing beats slow. (Bloukraanvoël)

CROWNED CRANE
Body and underwings grey; flight feathers black. Flies with neck outstretched and legs trailing.
(Mahem)

SECRETARYBIRD
Body and underwing coverts grey; flight feathers black; thighs black; tail grey, terminal bar black.
(Sekretarisvoël)

GYMNOGENE
Adult grey with black primaries and trailing edge; black tail with single white bar. Flaps slowly.
(Kaalwangvalk)

SOOTY FALCON
Entirely dark grey; flight feathers and tail darker; cere and feet yellow. Flies rapidly on slender wings.
(Roetvalk)

PALE CHANTING GOSHAWK
Above and below pale grey, secondaries whitish, primaries black, tail barred black and white. Legs red. Usually flies low.
(Bleeksingvalk)

DICKINSON'S KESTREL
Body grey; head very pale grey; underwing coverts grey; rest of wing and tail heavily barred. Flight swift and direct.
(Dickinsonse valk)

♂   ♀

DARK CHANTING GOSHAWK
Above and below dark grey, underwing coverts paler, primaries black, tail barred black and white. Legs red.
(Donkersingvalk)

♂

♀

EASTERN RED-FOOTED KESTREL
Male has grey body and undertail with chestnut vent; underwing coverts white; flight feathers black. Flight is gentle, may soar in wheeling flocks.
(Oostelike rooipootvalk)

WESTERN RED-FOOTED KESTREL
Male is entirely dark grey below except for chestnut vent. Flight is gentle, may soar in wheeling flocks.
(Westelike rooipootvalk)

BIRDS OF PREY WITH BARRED UNDERPARTS

Many of the small raptors, and a few of the larger ones too, have barred underbodies, underwings and undertails. Heavy barring is a difficult feature to see in a small, fast-flying bird since the barring cannot be properly distinguished. Many barred raptors, especially the sparrowhawks and goshawks, look confusingly similar, leaving one with the tantalising memory of an all-too-brief encounter. The best plan is rather to look for other, unique features of the flying bird and disregard the barring initially. The following notes are designed to draw attention to other important features that are worth watching for.

WESTERN BANDED SNAKE EAGLE
Body and underwing coverts grey; rest of wings white, well barred black; undertail white with single, broad black band (a second band is almost obscured by the undertail coverts). Soars. (Enkelbandslangarend)

SOUTHERN BANDED SNAKE EAGLE
Breast and underwing coverts grey; rest of wings well barred black; undertail banded black and white. Soars. (Dubbelbandslangarend)

CROWNED EAGLE
Body darkish; underwing coverts rufous; rest of wings white with two narrow black bars and broad black trailing edge; tail with three dark bands. (Kroonarend)

HONEY BUZZARD
A large raptor; body colour pale, dark or streaked. Underwings well barred plus dark carpal patches; undertail with two dark bands near the vent, plus one at the tip. Soars. (Wespedief)

RUFOUS-BREASTED SPARROWHAWK
Body and underwing coverts rufous; rest of underwings and tail well barred; soft parts yellow. Flight rapid.
(Rooiborssperwer)

OVAMBO SPARROWHAWK
Below well barred; above grey; dark tail with three pale bands, each band intersected with white feather shafts.
(Ovambosperwer)

LITTLE SPARROWHAWK
White throat, rest of underparts well barred rufous. Above grey, two conspicuous white spots on the upper tail. Soft parts yellow. Flight rapid.
(Kleinsperwer)

LITTLE BANDED GOSHAWK
All underparts well banded rufous; above plain grey.
(Gebande sperwer)

BLACK SPARROWHAWK
Large sparrowhawk; body black-and-white or mostly black; under-wings and tail white, well barred dark; eyes and legs yellow.
(Swartsperwer)

GABAR GOSHAWK
Breast grey; rest of underparts well barred; cere and legs red; eyes ruby-red; above grey with broad white rump. Flight rapid.
(Witkruissperwer)

AFRICAN GOSHAWK
Well barred rufous below; eyes and legs yellow. Above grey (male) or brown (female); two white spots on upper tail denote a male. Flight rapid unless in high morning display flight.
(Afrikaanse sperwer)

CUCKOO HAWK
Pale grey throat; rest of body and underwing coverts barred rufous; rest of wings barred brown; tail banded brown and white. Flies leisurely with slow wing beats.
(Koekoevalk)

MONTAGU'S HARRIER
Grey head and breast; belly white, streaked brown; underwings white with brown barring; primaries black; above grey with black primaries and thin black wing-bars. Flies low and slowly.
(Blouvleivalk)

LANNER FALCON
Body and underwing coverts lightly washed rufous; wings closely barred grey; undertail barred grey and white. Fast wing-flaps followed by brief glides; tail often spread.
(Edelvalk)

RED-NECKED FALCON
Below white; flanks and under-wing coverts washed rufous; all except throat closely barred black; tail with a broad, black subterminal band. Flight rapid.
(Rooinekvalk)

J.

PEREGRINE FALCON

Throat and upper breast white; rest of body and underwing coverts very pale rufous, closely barred black; tail well banded black. Fast wing-flaps followed by glides.
(Swerfvalk)

HOBBY FALCON

Body and underwing coverts washed rufous; thighs chestnut; underparts (except throat) heavily streaked and barred black. Flight rapid or leisurely. Summer.
(Europese boomvalk)

PYGMY FALCON

Very small (robin-sized) falcon. Body and underwing coverts white; underwings and tail black with dense white barring and banding. Flight rapid.
(Dwergvalk)

ROCK KESTREL

Below body rufous; rest white; flight feathers lightly barred grey; tail with broad, black subterminal band. Often hovers.
(Rooivalk)

LESSER KESTREL

Male has pale rufous body; underwings white; tail white with single, broad black terminal band. Female has entire underparts lightly streaked and barred black; tail with three narrow and one broad band. Small flocks wheel about in a leisurely manner. Summer.
(Kleinrooivalk)

EASTERN RED-FOOTED KESTREL (female)

Body, tail and underwings white, streaked and barred black; flight feathers much darker. Flocks of both sexes wheel about in a leisurely manner. Summer.
(Oostelike rooipootvalk)

glossary

The following terms have been used to describe birds in these pages

Band
A horizontal stripe of colour, as in tail-band.

Cap
The top of the head above the eyes.

Cere
The soft base of the beak in parrots, pigeons and birds of prey.

Coverts
The feathers that cover the ears, wings, etc.

Crown
The topmost part of the head.

Culmen
The top ridge of the bird's upper mandible.

Eye-stripe
A band of colour, often black, in front of and behind the eye.

Gape
The corner of the mouth where the mandibles are hinged.

Gular region
The sides of the throat.

Hood
The colouring of the top of the head when it extends to below the eyes.

Lores
The area between the eye and the beak.

Mandibles
The upper and lower jaws of a bird.

Mantle
The upper back adjacent to the lower back.

Moustacial streak
A line of colour extending from the bird's gape.

Nape
The back of the head.

Pectoral region
The sides of the upper breast.

Primaries
The major flight feathers on the outer part of the wing.

Rectrices
Tail feathers; rectrix in the singular.

Remiges
The primary flight feathers; remix in the singular.

Secondaries
The second most important flight feathers lying between the primary feathers and the body.

Streak
A vertical mark, longer than a spot.

Underwing coverts
The contour feathers covering the forward part of a bird's wing.

Thighs
The feathers covering a bird's upper legs.

Vent
The feathered region covering the bird's anus.

Afrikaans index

300 birds by colour

English index